CULTURES OF THE WORLD®

GUATEMALA

Sean Sheehan and Magdalene Koh

Marshall Cavendish
Benchmark

New York

PICTURE CREDITS

Cover photo: © John and Lisa Merrill / Danita Delimont Stock Photography
alt.TYPE / REUTERS: 25, 63, 70, 89, 123 • Corbis: 27, 28, 37, 46, 49, 55, 69, 88, 96, 105, 106, 110, 115, 126, 129 • David Simson: 35, 66, 79, 92, 95, 121, 127 • DDB Stock Photo: 17, 39, 42, 98, 100, 113 • Getty Images: 8, 18, 29, 31, 33, 44, 50, 51, 53, 54, 83, 84, 94, 99, 103, 108, 109, 117, 118, 120 • Guatemala Tourist Commission: 13 • Hutchison Library: 14, 73, 86 • Lonely Planet Images: 68, 76, 87, 90, 124 • National Geographic: 1, 5, 21, 57, 93 • Nik Wheeler: 3, 64, 82, 104 • North Wind Picture Archives: 23, 24, 32 • Photolibrary: 6, 7, 10, 20, 22, 30, 36, 43, 47, 48, 52, 58, 59, 71, 80, 81, 85, 91, 97, 102, 111, 112, 114, 125, 130, 131 • South American Pictures: 4, 9, 16, 19, 41, 62, 65, 74, 75, 77, 78, 107, 116, 119, 122 • Sue Cunningham Photographic: 38, 45, 61

PRECEDING PAGE

Guatemalan women dress up in their traditional outfits for a village festival.

Publisher (U.S.): Michelle Bisson
Editors: Deborah Grahame, Mindy Pang
Copyreader: Daphne Hougham
Designer: Geoslyn Lim
Cover picture researcher: Connie Gardner
Picture researcher: Thomas Khoo

Marshall Cavendish Benchmark
99 White Plains Road
Tarrytown, NY 10591
Web site: www.marshallcavendish.us

© Times Media Private Limited 1998
© Marshall Cavendish International (Asia) Private Limited 2010
® "Cultures of the World" is a registered trademark of Times Publishing Limited.

Originated and designed by Times Media Private Limited
An imprint of Marshall Cavendish International (Asia) Private Limited
A member of Times Publishing Limited

Marshall Cavendish is a trademark of Times Publishing Limited.

All Internet sites were correct and accurate at the time of printing. All monetary figures in this publication are in U.S. dollars.

Library of Congress Cataloging-in-Publication Data

Sheehan, Sean, 1951-
    Guatemala / by Sean Sheehan and Magdalene Koh. — 2nd ed.
        p. cm.
    Includes bibliographical references and index.
    Summary: "Provides comprehensive information on the geography, history,
        wildlife, governmental structure, economy, cultural diversity, peoples,
        religion, and culture of Guatemala"--Provided by publisher.
    ISBN 978-0-7614-3412-2   3321 9084
        1. Guatemala—Juvenile literature. [1. Guatemala.] I. Koh, Magdalene. II.
    Title.
    F1463.2.S5 2009
    972.81—dc22   2008028787

Printed in China
7 6 5 4 3 2 1

CONTENTS

Locally handwoven head masks for sale at a Guatemalan market.

Bright colors and embroidery characterize Guatemalan handicrafts.

INTRODUCTION

STEP INTO GUATEMALA AND enter a different world. There, smoldering volcanoes meet swirling mists, and fertile coastal plains enfold lush green cloud forests. Nature's tropical colors are reflected in the rainbow hues of the indigenous attire. Despite its awesome natural beauty, Guatemala bears a legacy of much violence and bloodshed.

More than a decade after signing the 1996 Peace Accords, the country is now emerging from the shadows of Latin America's longest civil war. Foreign investments are flowing in, boosting long-term development. Guatemalans are enjoying better educational prospects, but unequal wealth distribution, disparate economic opportunities, and inadequate health care continue to disable social cohesion. Escalating crime rates are another worry. Nonetheless, the resilience of its people—heirs to the ancient Maya, one of the greatest civilizations in the world—has stood the test of time. As stability dawns, Guatemalans confront their future with renewed hopes for a better tomorrow.

GEOGRAPHY

GUATEMALA IS THE THIRD-LARGEST country in Central America. Spanning a total area of 42,042 square miles (108,890 square km), it is slightly smaller than Tennessee. The country shares a border to the north and west with Mexico and one with Belize on the northeast. Honduras and El Salvador lie to its southeast. The Caribbean Sea edges a short coastline on the northeast, and the Pacific Ocean stretches for 150 miles (241 km) along the southwestern coast.

Guatemala has three distinct geographic regions: the volcanic highlands, the lowlands, and a coastal plain south of the mountains. About 60 percent of the population lives in the volcanic uplands and along the coastal region. The rest remain clustered around the Petén area in the mountains to the north of the volcanic uplands. Guatemala has a higher population density than any other Latin American country.

The 1976 earthquake affected 8 percent of Guatemala's territory, killing about 23,000 people and leaving 20 percent of the population homeless.

Left: **A dramatic image of the erupting Pacaya volcano. Located in a region of volcanic activity, Guatemala enjoys some of the world's most scenic landscapes.**

Opposite: **The picturesque Lake Atitlán in Guatemala's highlands.**

7

Children playing on a dock on Lake Atitlán.

HIGHLANDS

Lying above 1,000 feet (305 m), the highlands occupy about half of Guatemala's total land area. This elevated land cuts across the country, from the southeast to the northwest, for a distance of 180 miles (290 km). The southern range of mountains, the Sierra Madre, includes over 30 volcanic peaks that stretch down from southern Mexico. They include the country's highest mountain, Tajumulco, at 13,815 feet (4,211 m). Some of the volcanoes are active and some are dormant. Major earthquakes occurred in 1717, 1773, 1917, and 1976. In 2007, two earthquakes measuring 6.8 and 5.9 on the Richter scale of magnitude struck within the same week. Fortunately, no deaths or major damage were reported.

The central highland is traversed by two main rivers separating the southern volcanic landscape from other mountains, or sierras, to the north. The Motagua River flows toward the Caribbean, while the Cuilco River runs westward. Rivers in the northern region tend to flow north across a part of Mexico into the Gulf of Mexico. There are two large lakes on the southern side of the highlands, Lake Atitlán and Lake Amatitlán.

The picturesque highland scenery is dotted with ancient Mayan towns that proudly preserve Indian culture. Most of the locals there are farmers, growing corn and vegetables in the valleys the way their pre-Columbian ancestors did. Unfortunately, like their predecessors, they have to deal with the region's earthquake threat.

Most cities and towns are situated in Guatemala's southern half. Apart from a few coastal settlements, the highlands are the most populated areas.

LOWLANDS

The Petén lowlands, with an elevation between 500 and 700 feet (152 and 213 m), form part of a fairly level limestone shelf that includes Yucatán in Mexico. Limestone is easy to cut and is ideal for making plaster. These properties of limestone were artistically exploited by the Maya while making Petén their civilization's heartland. Some of the most spectacular ancient Mayan cities are located in this region, although many more probably remain undiscovered, buried in the area's thick rain forests. Natural caves are formed in limestone regions, and the Maya treated them as holy places. This is vividly depicted in the murals and texts uncovered in Naj Tanuch Cave, which was discovered in 1980. Interestingly, the limestone landscape has very few rivers because most of the rainfall drains underground through the porous limestone.

Guatemala's history, like its geography, has been greatly influenced by the large number of earthquakes that strike the country. The Sierra Madre includes 33 volcanic peaks, many of which are still active.

A parcel of land being cleared by slash-and-burn tactics to make a farm. Guatemala still retains a vast expanse of natural rain forest, but the rapidly increasing population leads to more tracts of land being cleared for agriculture.

Petén covers almost one-third of Guatemala but does not support much of the population because it is not suited for agriculture. Typically, people who move to Petén use slash-and-burn methods to wrest a living from farming. Although about 90 percent of Petén is still covered with primary forest, this figure will steadily decline if the slash-and-burn method continues.

The region's isolation and low population have enabled wildlife to flourish. Over 300 species of birds have been found. Valuable forests with mahogany, rubber trees, and tropical cedar are common. Land surrounding the main town of Flores is used for sugarcane and fruit cultivation. The town itself fronts on Lake Petén Itzá, an Indian area that was not conquered by the Spanish until the end of the 17th century.

COASTAL PLAIN

Guatemala's Pacific littoral—a region lying along a shore—boasts a spectacular landscape. The volcanic slopes drop close to the sea, forming beachs of black volcanic sand. That area is characterized by mangrove swamps and rich alluvial soil, which easily nourishes a fertile plain up to 45 miles (72 km) wide and 150 miles (241 km) long. Grass grows easily there, and cattle ranches thrive alongside numerous coffee, sugar, cacao, cotton, soybean, sorghum, and fruit plantations. Despite the constant threat of earthquakes and volcanic eruptions, the capital—Guatemala City—and other major cities are situated on this plain.

The coastal plain also includes Lake Izabal—the largest lake in the country. The Pacific Ocean supports a small tuna, shrimp, and mackerel fishing industry, while the sandy shore attracts sea turtles in search of nests for their eggs.

Bathers along the palm tree-edged beach of Lake Izabal in Livingston.

LAKE ATITLÁN

Lake Atitlán, measuring 12 miles by 6 miles (19 km by 10 km), occupies a volcanic crater. With depths of more than 1,000 feet (305 m), it is the deepest lake in Central America. Its backdrop of surrounding hills and the volcanic mountains of Atitlán, San Pedro, and Tolimán provide a picture-perfect setting, thus making Lake Atitlán one of Guatemala's most popular tourist destinations. A number of rivers run into the lake, but there is no visible outlet. In this respect, Lake Atitlán is similar to Utah's Great Salt Lake, but unlike its American counterpart, the water is not salty. This feature suggests that there are underground channels linking the lake to the Pacific Ocean through which water drains away. When the water in lakes is lost through evaporation, it turns salty, much like that found in the Great Salt Lake.

Arable land, including meadows and pastures, occupies about 25 percent of Guatemala's total land area. Another 40 percent consists of forests and woodlands.

CLIMATE

Although Guatemala lies in the tropics, its climate varies depending on the regional elevation and its proximity to the coast. From sea level to around 6,000 feet (1,830 m), daytime temperatures range between 77°F and 86°F (25°C and 30°C). Nights are usually chilly but not terribly cold. Most of the country's major towns are situated within these altitudes. Daytime temperature, however, in places over 7,000 feet (2,135 m) can drop to as low as 52°F (11°C). In the highlands, night temperature sometimes plunges to freezing level. The lowlands are hot and steamy, with heavy rain in the summer but little precipitation during the dry season.

The months between November and April are considered the driest period, but both the Pacific and Caribbean coastal areas remain humid and rainy throughout the year. Rainfall varies from 80 inches (203 cm) in the highlands to less than half that amount in the driest season. Tropical storms sometimes occur during September and October.

A varied climate such as this is economically beneficial because virtually every variety of crop that can be grown in the Western Hemisphere is cultivated some place or another in Guatemala.

CITIES

The capital of Guatemala used to be Antigua, but an earthquake in 1773 virtually destroyed the town. A new capital, Guatemala City, was founded three years later in a neighboring highland valley. The new capital withstood several natural disasters, such as the series of destructive earthquakes in 1917 and 1918. Instead of establishing yet another new capital, Guatemalans decided to rebuild the town. Today about one in five Guatemalans lives in the capital, accounting for half the country's urban population, thereby making Guatemala City, with its 2.5 million inhabitants, the largest Central American city except for Mexico City.

As Guatemala's economic, political, and cultural hub, the capital continues to grow and influence many aspects of national life. It is not an especially attractive city, nor does it enjoy a rich cultural history. While glistening skyscrapers dominate the city center, shanty dwellings often lie in their shadow.

Quezaltenango is Guatemala's second-largest city. It is also situated in the highlands, some distance west of the capital. It became prosperous during the 19th century's coffee boom, but a 1902 earthquake left it in ruins. Although it was later rebuilt, many families had already moved to Guatemala City. Compared with the capital, Quezaltenango has a provincial atmosphere, but its architecture is more interesting. It is a popular destination for international visitors.

Other important Guatemalan towns include Chichicastenango, where the majority of the people are Mayan Indian, and ancient Antigua, the old colonial capital. The latter's impressive architecture dates back to the Spanish occupation. Both towns have unique characters and offer fascinating insights into Guatemalan history.

Guatemala City, the capital of Guatemala and the center of business and trade, lights up the evening sky.

13

Slash-and-burn clearing of rain forests such as these for agriculture still continues in spite of the environmental dangers it poses.

THE RAIN FOREST

Guatemala's most precious resource is its vast stretches of tropical rain forests. More than 700 types of trees rise over 100 feet (30 m) to form a thick canopy overhead. At ground level, some 4,000 types of flowering plants have been identified. New plant species that are not found anywhere else in the world continue to be discovered in Guatemala.

These rain forests are valuable resources for modern medical research. Recent explorations have yielded treatments for many illnesses and diseases, and it is thought that many more potential cures are just waiting to be found. Wild yams growing in the forest have provided medical scientists with important medicines, and a species of frogs has produced a powerful anesthetic. There have been heated debates over the use of the rain forest for these purposes, with some arguing that foreign drug companies are exploiting the forests for financial gain without sharing their profits with the country or its inhabitants. New laws are being considered that will ensure local participation in all future research activities.

A report in 1990 claimed that 40 percent of the country's forest cover had been lost since 1960. Meanwhile, land clearing for farming continues to eat away at those heritage reserves. With the help of international ecological groups, Guatemala has set up many national parks, the most ambitious being the Maya Biosphere Reserve. It covers an area of over 4 million acres (1.62 million ha) in northern Petén and was established with the intention of preserving the tropical rain forest. The reserve consists of an uninhabited core area that is surrounded by small farms whose inhabitants are engaged in sustainable agriculture—farming that does not use up or damage the resource.

In practice, nevertheless, land conservation is threatened by an influx of Guatemalans settling in Petén. Refugees returning to their native land after the 36-year civil war are also adding pressure to the terrain. Areas within the reserve are being allocated to refugees. Such relocation worsens the rapid spread of slash-and-burn farming, which leads to further depletion of the rain forest. Illegal logging, often organized in Mexico, poses another serious problem.

AMPHIBIAN VISITORS

During the night, forests come alive with the chorus of frogs. Campers in the outdoors may be startled by the appearance of the red-eyed tree frog in their tents. This beautiful and harmless pale green amphibian is smaller than the size of a person's thumb. A less savory guest is the giant marine toad, the largest toad in the Americas. Weighing in excess of 2 pounds (1 kg) and measuring more than 8 inches (20.32 cm) in length, its toxins can cause hallucinations. During religious ceremonies, the ancient Maya often licked the toad's glands and interpreted the induced visions to beholders.

A jaguar in the trees of the Guatemalan rain forest regards the photographer at work warily.

WILDLIFE

Guatemala enjoys great wildlife diversity. Jaguars—the largest of all cat species found in the Americas—lurk more abundantly in the Petén rain forest than anywhere else in Central America. These beautiful endangered animals were revered by the ancient Maya, who saw them as natural symbols of power and stealth. The Maya carved images of the jaguar on stone and worshiped them as gods.

Like the jaguar, the puma—also known as the cougar or panther—is a forest cat that is rarely seen. It is a solitary animal that can grow to over 9 feet (2.7 m) in length, of which one-third is the tail.

Perhaps the best-known reptile found in Guatemala is the boa constrictor. This snake is not poisonous, but as its name suggests, it will squeeze the life out of its prey before swallowing the animal whole—a full plate. There are 15 species of poisonous snakes in Guatemala; one of the most common is the small but very deadly fer-de-lance, a type of pit viper. Villagers fear these far more than the huge boa constrictors because the fer-de-lance's favorite food, the common mouse, draws the snake close to their settlements.

Birdlife is extraordinarily colorful and fascinating, especially in Guatemala's tropical rain forests. Varieties of parrots make themselves heard as well as seen. Tiny hummingbirds share the same habitat as the long-tailed quetzals, which can exceed 4 feet (1.2 m) in length. The brilliantly colored quetzal is Guatemala's national bird, and a reserve has been set aside near Cobán in an effort to protect it from poachers and habitat destruction. The country's most unusual bird is the *oropéndola*, which weaves a long nest that hangs conspicuously from trees and even from telephone lines.

Guatemala's short Caribbean coastline is home to the manatee, a slow-moving aquatic mammal that resembles a seal but is most closely related to the elephant. Manatees were once commonly spotted off the coast of Florida. Their eyesight is poor, but they are able to communicate by muzzle-to-muzzle contact. They live alone or in groups, and sometimes the groups come together to form herds. Unfortunately, the manatee has been overhunted for its meat and oil, so much so that it has now become an increasingly rare sight.

The mangroves along the Pacific shore are important wildlife habitats. They attract a variety of animal and birdlife, including the white ibis, the great jabiru (a large stork), raccoon, and opossum. The mangroves also provide shelter and breeding grounds for fish and crustaceans. Additionally, they form vital feeding and nesting areas for wading birds.

The scarlet macaw, an endangered species, is one of the many types of parrots found in Guatemala.

17

HISTORY

HUMAN HABITATION IN THE AMERICAS began around 60,000 years ago when the first humans reached North America by crossing the Bering Strait from Asia. These early hunter-gatherers gradually worked their way south into Central America, leaving the beginnings of many cultures in their long journey. When the climate began to warm, between 11,000 and 6000 B.C., the stage was set for the rise of agriculture.

There is evidence that Guatemala was inhabited around 9000 B.C. By about 5000 B.C. cave dwellers in Central America started cultivating grasses. The cultivation of corn would soon follow. By 2600 B.C. pre-Maya people settled in the region that is now known as Guatemala, and some 500 years later, the first farming settlements were established around lakes and rivers.

Little is known about the earliest inhabitants of Guatemala. This has encouraged various unproven and often outlandish theories involving early settlers from Egypt, Phoenicia, Cambodia, the "lost" kingdom of Atlantis, and even aliens from outer space.

Above: **A Mayan funerary urn in the shape of a face mask. It dates back to the eighth century A.D.**

Opposite: **An open court-yard of the venerable Santa Clara Church in Antigua, Guatemala's first capital.**

PRE-CLASSIC MAYA

By 1500 B.C. settled communities had developed. Archaeological discoveries suggest that these people worshipped fertility figures. They grew corn and vegetables, slept in hammocks, and began using cocoa beans as money. Between 800 and 500 B.C. the number of settlements increased substantially. It is likely that certain aspects of early Mayan culture in the highlands, such as writing, calendar making, and art forms, were influenced by the Olmec and Izapan civilizations in what is present-day Mexico.

The ancient Mayan ruins of North Acropolis in Tikal.

The earliest Maya homes were rectangular. Built of mud and straw, they were set on earthen platforms raised above the ground to protect inhabitants from heavy rainfall. This basic design would later be used in the construction of the great Mayan pyramid temples.

In the lowlands, the non-Mayan Chicanel culture's interest in architecture was passionately developed by the Maya. Just how the various influences came to bear on Mayan culture will probably never be known. But by around A.D. 300, at a time when the Roman Empire was entering terminal decline, the Mayan civilization blossomed in a way that continues to fascinate and astonish historians. Some archaeologists refer to this renaissance as the Maya Fluorescence.

THE MAYAN GOLDEN AGE

Mayan civilization reached its height between A.D. 300 and 900. The magnitude of its amazing cultural richness can be seen in its architecture, art, mathematics, astronomy, and writing that have managed to survive. Tikal, located in the Petén region, appears to have been the cultural capital of the Mayan world, but another possible site is El Mirador. Found in the far north of Guatemala, it is the site of the largest pyramids the Maya ever built. Some of what is known about Mayan culture comes from the accounts of Spanish missionaries, who took a scholarly interest in the beliefs and practices that they were intent on eliminating.

Mayan thought was most advanced in the field of astronomy. Considerable effort was devoted to plotting the movements of the sun, moon, and especially Venus. The Maya could predict eclipses and may have studied other planets in our solar system. Considering the fact that their calculations were made without any of the technology available to modern astronomers, the Maya were incredibly accurate. Only 7 minutes separate their lunar cycle from ours, and they plotted the course of Venus with a margin of error that amounts to just 2 hours in 500 years. Their mathematics included the notion of zero, a concept that reached Europe from the East only during the Middle Ages.

The ancient Maya were a militaristic people. Young males were separated from their families and brought up as a group that was well versed in the arts of war. They made constant raids into neighboring communities, and prisoners were taken as slaves or were ritually killed. There is evidence suggesting that different cities formed alliances through marriage.

Excavations have shown Tikal to be the most advanced Mayan city in the sixth century. Tikal covered an area of 6 square miles (15.5 square km), with an estimated population of 10,000 to 40,000. Some 3,000 buildings, ranging from splendid temples to lowly huts, have been identified. Other Mayan "cities" would have been smaller but similar in concept: dispersed clusters of peasant homes surrounding a temple that served as the center of communal activities.

Temple interiors and exteriors were vividly painted, as proven by a few fragments still bearing the original pigments. These buildings were focal points for a sophisticated culture that was far more advanced than any European city of that time.

This 2,000-year-old wall painting is the oldest intact Mayan mural ever found. The mural depicts the first known portrayal of the corn god's journey from the underworld to Earth.

The Spanish influence on Guatemalan culture is evident in the architecture of old cities.

UNEXPLAINED MYSTERY

The year A.D. 889 was a significant date in the Mayan calendar as it indicates the end of their flourishing culture. Important dates normally were marked in numerous stone inscriptions, yet only three commemorative stelae (inscribed stone pillars) have been found bearing this date. Historians use this as partial evidence suggesting that around A.D. 800 the Mayan civilization began the collapse that lasted for over a century. No recorded dates have been found after the 10th century, when great temples and palaces were abandoned to the jungle's mercy.

No explanation has ever been found for this dramatic demise, but numerous hypotheses have been suggested. These include earthquakes, an invasion from Mexico, a social uprising, agricultural disaster, and rampant disease. The truth may never be known. Perhaps a number of factors combined to bring this major civilization to an end. By the time the Spanish arrived, the great Mayan cities had been deserted for almost 500 years.

THE SPANISH CONQUEST

The arrival of the Spanish in the early 16th century proved to be a momentous event in Guatemalan history. The terms pre-Conquest or pre-Columbian are often used in Guatemalan history and culture to refer to the period before the Spanish conquest.

In 1524, three years after the conquest of the Aztecs in Mexico, Hernán (or Hernando) Cortés sent an army of some 400 Spanish and 200 Mexican soldiers into Guatemala under the command of Pedro de Alvarado. A strong Indian army of 30,000 was unable to defeat the Spanish, who had the advantage of superior military technology. Besides swords, crossbows, metal armor, and gunpowder, the Spanish used a type of heavy portable matchlock gun known as a harquebus that was supported on a tripod for ease of firing.

The Spanish also unwittingly brought another weapon in the form of European diseases, which the Maya had no immunity against. In some areas, over half of the original population died after contracting smallpox, influenza, and measles.

Eldorado—from the Spanish word for gold—was an imagined land of riches that drew the conquistadors to the Americas. They never found their golden dream in Guatemala. Instead, many settled down to the business of shipping commodities such as cotton, tobacco, and chocolate back to Spain. The Spanish established their capital at Antigua, the first planned city in the Americas, but an earthquake destroyed it in 1773.

Over two centuries of colonial rule left its mark on Guatemalan society. Antigua and Guatemala City were founded by the Spanish. The Roman Catholic religion, Spanish language, and a pro-Spanish social hierarchy have remained as legacies of the Spanish presence. The Indian culture, however, was not eradicated. It survived, to a large extent, by absorbing aspects of Spanish culture without sacrificing the older Mayan beliefs.

The Roman Catholic Church presided over the destruction of native idols and set about converting the Indian population to Catholicism.

The history of Mayan civilization has been divided into three main periods: the Pre-Classic (2000 B.C.–A.D. 300), the Classic (A.D. 300–900), and the Post-Classic (A.D. 900–1521).

23

THE POWER OF THE CHURCH

In the wake of Alvarado's conquest, the Franciscans were the first Roman Catholic religious order to reach Guatemala, followed by the Dominicans and then the Jesuits. They were granted large tracts of Indian land and soon became wealthy and powerful. In 1572 an office of the Inquisition was established in Antigua to point out and punish those who declined to convert to Christianity. By the mid-18th century, the Church's power was beginning to rival that of the Spanish government. To curtail their growing influence, the authorities decided to take certain steps, and in 1767, the Jesuits were banned from Guatemala and other Spanish colonies.

In the early history of Spanish rule, the priests sometimes achieved what the army found impossible. In Verapaces, an area to the north of Guatemala City, the indigenous Achi Indians resisted the Spanish so stubbornly that Alvarado's forces gave up the attempt and retreated. A group of Dominican priests was left to pacify the Indians and succeeded without the use of force.

A Franciscan or Grey Friar.   A Grey Friar or Cordelier without his Mantle.

A STRUGGLE FOR POWER

Foreign rule over Guatemala came to a quiet end in 1821 when it declared independence from Spain. Spain, suffering from domestic economic and political problems, relinquished all its interests in the New World. In 1823 Guatemala joined the new United Provinces of Central America. It was the only time that all of Central America was united as one nation, and Guatemala City became the capital of this confederation. For the Indians, though, little had changed—their Spanish rulers were simply replaced by Ladinos, the Spanish-American elite. Indians were not granted citizenship in the United Provinces of Central America, leaving the social and political imbalances firmly in place.

A conflict emerged in the new confederation between left-wing and right-wing interests. Under the leadership of Rafael Carrera, Guatemala was declared an independent and sovereign state in 1847. In 1873 a charismatic military leader, Rufino Barrios, became president of Guatemala and initiated liberal reforms that angered the conservative church. Unused land

Previous dictator and ruling party presidential candidate, retired General José Efraín Ríos Montt, speaking at a rally.

Juan José Arévalo described his politics as "spiritual socialism." He introduced sweeping economic and political reforms that gave land and ensured human rights to Indians. At every turn Arévalo was beset by attempted military coups. His elected successor, Colonel Jacobo Arbenz Guzmán, was another reformer who challenged the United Fruit Company's economic stranglehold. Arbenz's government turned over 2 billion acres of land to small farmers, and this included the unused land owned by United Fruit.

In 1954 the United States government, citing Communist influences within the Arbenz government, intervened with a military invasion of Guatemala. Code-named Operation SUCCESS and planned by the Central Intelligence Agency (CIA), previously classified records that were released in May 1997 disclosed how the CIA had considered assassinating Arbenz. It was feared that Guatemala would become the then Soviet Union's ally unless something were done to break the chain of events. The assassination did not take place, however. Arbenz fled to Cuba and went into exile in Mexico. Power passed into the hands of the army.

Under President Jimmy Carter, the United States withdrew military and financial support for the Guatemalan government. The Ronald Reagan administration, however, restored military aid under Guatemalan dictator General José Efraín Ríos Montt in 1982.

belonging to the church was confiscated and sold to German immigrants to grow coffee. Barrios was excommunicated by the pope. He responded by exiling the archbishop of Guatemala, a move that effectively closed down the churches. Before his assassination in 1885, Barrios was already reviled as a tyrant. He confiscated Maya lands and forced Indians into a system of compulsory labor on coffee plantations.

The next 60 years witnessed a power struggle that involved countless military coups, dictators, and the growing power of the U.S.-owned United Fruit Company. During this time, only two leaders managed to remain in office for consecutive terms, and both of them were thought to be unstable characters. In 1944 popular discontent forced Jorge Ubico—a tyrant who ruled for 14 years and believed himself to be a reincarnation of Napoleon—out of office. In the following year, Guatemala's most democratic elections took place, and Juan José Arévalo became president after winning 85 percent of the votes. The new mood of reform became so popular that the change of power was hailed as "The 1944 Revolution."

MILITARY RULE AND CIVIL WAR

Guatemala was torn by political divisions between the right-wing faction, which supported traditional ruling interests, and the left-wing group, which fought for social reform. Increasing numbers of peasants formed a guerrilla opposition in protest against governments that supported the United Fruit Company, thus sowing the seeds for future conflict.

The civil war started in 1960 when the military launched a campaign of terrorism and slaughter. During Colonel Arana Osorio's presidency in the 1970s, an estimated 15,000 Guatemalans were killed by military death squads. General elections continued to take place, but it was the military leaders who assumed political power. Some 25,000 Guatemalans were killed during the Romeo Lucas García presidency that began in 1978.

PEACE AT LAST

The 1990-elected government offered to investigate the human rights abuses, but corruption persisted and dissidents continued to "disappear." A group of Norwegian mediators started a peace process that eventually led to the end of Guatemala's civil war. Public demonstrations helped to establish a new government in 1994 and boosted the country's peace prospects. The following year, 1995, was declared El Año de la Maya (The Year of the Maya) when the military and the guerrillas began to discuss a lasting peace settlement.

New elections were held in 1996, but over 60 percent of the electorate did not stir itself to vote. The new Alvaro Arzú government pursued peace talks, and in December 1996 the adversaries in Latin America's longest civil war agreed on a permanent cease-fire. A conflict that had lasted 36 years, claiming 200,000 lives, had finally ended.

Jacobo Arbenz Guzmán (*center*) was ousted as president of Guatemala in an anticommunist revolt.

27

GOVERNMENT

A NEW ERA IN GUATEMALAN politics began when Alvaro Arzú was elected as president in 1996. His party, the National Advancement Party (PAN), won just over half the vote, narrowly defeating another right-wing party—the Guatemalan Republican Front (FRG). In a way, it was not a great victory for democracy because 63 percent of the electorate had abstained from voting. Yet the election was significant because Arzú committed his government to peace talks with the Guatemalan National Revolutionary Unit (URNG)—the armed guerrilla opposition.

Under the terms of the Peace Accords the army was required to relinquish its domestic security role to a new police force. In a democracy, the armed forces' defense of the country from external threats is considered nonpolitical. The people hoped that the new agreement would free Guatemala from the recurrent threat of military dictatorship. Various paramilitary groups that were involved in systematic human rights abuses have been abolished. In the treaty's immediate aftermath, the government closed five military bases. The United Nations also approved the deployment of a military mission to supervise the disarmament and demobilization of URNG soldiers in early 1997.

Above: **Guatemalan presidential candidate Rigoberta Menchu casts her vote during the 2007 general elections in Guatemala.**

Opposite: **The Central Square government office building in Guatemala City.**

THE CONSTITUTION

The constitution, which came into effect in 1986, remains the bedrock for governance. Guatemala is defined constitutionally as a democratic republic, with power being divided among the legislative, executive, and judiciary branches.

The city hall at Sololá, Guatemala.

The legislature is responsible for drafting and passing laws. Called the National Congress, its members are elected every four years by popular vote. During the 2003 election, the number of congressional seats increased from 113 to 158. The National Congress is a unicameral legislature, which means that there is just one chamber, not two as in the United States and elsewhere.

Executive power rests with the president, who is directly elected by universal suffrage, and the vice president. Individuals campaigning for the presidency, vice presidency, or a seat in Congress must belong to and have been nominated by authorized political parties. The main restriction on the authorization of political parties is that they must not advocate the overthrow of the democratic process. The judiciary, concerned with courts of law and the interpretation of laws, is ruled by the Supreme Court of Justice. The Supreme Court consists of 13 justices, each of whom is elected to a five-year position.

For the purposes of administration, the country is divided into 22 *departamentos* (de-par-tuh-MEN-tos), each of which elects its own governor. Petén, for example, is a department divided into a number of

SHARING LOCAL GOVERNMENT

In predominantly Indian regions, the local government often takes two separate forms: one for the Indian population and another for the Ladinos. For example, the town of Chichicastenango has two sets of local officials. The central government appoints officers, but Indians elect their own civil officials. The locally elected Indian government has its own mayor and its own court for dealing with offenses committed by local Indians.

municipalities that operate through elected councils and are headed by different mayors. Independent candidates who are not affiliated with a political party are allowed to run for office at this level.

THE PRESIDENT

The president of Guatemala is elected for a single four-year term. During that time, the president is the head of state and head of government. A president does not always need the support of a majority of the population in order to get elected. For example, universal suffrage was abolished by the military in the 1950s, and only half of the new electorate voted during the1970 election when Colonel Carlos Arana Osorio polled just under half of those votes. This meant that very few Guatemalans voted for their new president. A similar situation occurred during the 1996 elections.

According to the constitution, the army has no political role, but politics has played a very big part in Guatemala's recent history. Between 1954—when a democratically elected government was overthrown—and the 1990s, a number of Guatemala's presidents have been army officers.

Guatemalan president Álvaro Colom Caballeros started his term in January 2008.

THE FIRST GOVERNOR OF GUATEMALA

Pedro de Alvarado was a deputy to Hernán (or Hernando) Cortés, the Spanish conqueror of Mexico. The 39-year-old was sent to the south in 1523 to claim Indian territory for the Spanish Crown, establish and promote the Catholic faith among the pagan natives, and confiscate as much gold as possible. Mayan history records a legendary personal duel between Alvarado and an Indian king, Tecún Umán, in which the Spaniard emerged victorious. Alvarado's commission was aided by European diseases such as measles and smallpox, because the Indians had no natural resistance to these infections. It took Alvarado more than six years to gain control over Guatemala, though he established a capital close to Antigua within three years of arriving. He had his own palace built by captured Indians working as slave laborers. Alvarado's reputation for cruelty got him recalled to Spain at one point, but he later returned and ruled Guatemala as his personal kingdom. He piled up an enormous amount of wealth, but he found no serenity, as his restless nature drove him first to Peru and then to Mexico, where he died in 1541.

Upon hearing of her husband's death, Alvarado's wife, Beatriz de la Cueva, is said to have ordered the palace in Antigua to be painted black both inside and out. She also proclaimed herself the governess, but within the span of one day, an earthquake-triggered mud slide hit the whole city and buried all. Beatriz de la Cueva governed for all of 24 hours, becoming the first, and as yet, the only woman to rule Guatemala.

THE ARMY

The army has played an infamous role in Guatemalan politics. After the military coup in 1954, power passed into the hands of the country's army. Over the next 30 years, the country suffered violent divisions, both socially and politically. Conservative groups—consisting of the pro-business parties and large landowners, who distrusted democracy because they thought it would weaken their economic power—turned to the military to suppress all political opposition. The army pursued this agenda so ruthlessly that their disregard for human rights shocked most of the world. Colonel Osorio, who ruled from 1970 to 1974, declared: "If it is necessary to turn the country into a cemetery in order to pacify it, I will not hesitate to do so."

Under the 1996 Peace Accords, there was a reduction of 46,000 troops in the army. Its budget was also heavily cut. A United Nations report concluded that the military government was responsible for 93 percent of human rights violations in Guatemala. It remains uncertain, however, whether the army officers who committed violent crimes against civilians will be adequately brought to justice. Many perpetrators have been acquitted. The 2005 Amnesty International Report records that human rights abuses by the armed forces continue to be a problem in Guatemala.

In line with new curbs on the army's political power, the role of the police force was also redefined. Once considered an instrument of the ruling party, the police are now more concerned with the justice system than with politics. Guatemala's move toward democracy has been aided by Central America's recent stability. The citizens hope that new economic opportunities will improve the lives of all Guatemalans and carve out new roles for the army and the police in protecting and upholding the masses instead of oppressing them, as had been customary.

Armed Guatemalan soldiers parading during a ceremony.

A MILITARY DICTATOR

General Enrique Peralta Azurdia (1908–97) was a military dictator in the 1960s. Although he has largely been forgotten by most Guatemalans today, his career typifies the military's role in Guatemalan politics.

Elections were due to be held in 1964. On March 29, 1963, Juan José Arévalo Bermejo (1904–2008) returned to Guatemala from his exile in Argentina. Arévalo was famous as the liberal reformer and civilian president whose tenure in the 1950s modernized the country. His arrival scared the ruling conservative groups, who feared that Arévalo might win the election. General Peralta, however, headed a successful coup that took place on March 30 and wrested power from Arévalo. Peralta organized his own death squads. Other political parties soon discovered that it was too dangerous to oppose him. Organizers of trade unions simply "disappeared." When elections finally took place in 1966, the main civilian candidate was assassinated.

Bishop Juan Gerardi was beaten to death in 1998 after he published a study detailing the military's involvement in most of the cases concerning Guatemala's human rights abuses.

THE OPPOSITION

The only alternative voices against the Guatemalan government until 1996 were the various groups operating as armed guerrillas. For over 35 years, such groups were supported mainly by the Indians and were excluded from mainstream politics. Early guerrilla groups were called the Guerrilla Army of the Poor and the Organization of the People in Arms, but over time, the Guatemalan National Revolutionary Unit (URNG) emerged as the main opposition to the harsh government.

The political fracturing of Guatemalan society began in 1960. Disillusioned with widespread corruption and incompetence in the government, two army officers fled to the eastern highlands. They were soon joined by other equally alienated groups. By the end of the 1960s, the first wave of armed opposition had been virtually defeated, but brutal military rule throughout the 1970s ignited renewed opposition. Demands for human rights and social justice fell on deaf ears, and officials who did not support the military were murdered. In the cities, large numbers of politicians, academics, priests, trade unionists, teachers, and lawyers were killed. In the countryside, even larger numbers of indigenous Indians were slaughtered. Between 1978 and 1982 the army wiped out an estimated 25,000 Indians. The brutal suppression of political opponents became so blatant that the United States, under President Jimmy Carter, suspended military aid to the Guatemalan government in 1977. Such aid was restored in 1982, under President Ronald Regan.

The imprisonment and murder of political opponents continued throughout the 1980s and well into the 1990s. Under the terms of the 1996 Peace Accords, the URNG was required to hand over all its weapons and disband its 3,000 members. It seems likely that at least one new political party in the future will announce itself as the peacetime heir to the URNG. Early in 1997, the United Nations sent military observers to Guatemala to oversee the disarmament and demobilization of the guerrilla army that had withstood the government forces for 36 years.

A decade later, Guatemala has experienced successive democratic elections. Having acknowledged its role in human rights violations during the civil war, the government is making compensatory payments to families of civilians who were killed in those circumstances by the military. Nonetheless, little progress has been made in prosecuting former soldiers and human rights violators. A matter of grave concern is that violent crimes against women are escalating. Amnesty International noted that many victims were murdered or mutilated with no apparent motives.

Guatemala's coat of arms is placed proudly on their national flag.

THE NATIONAL FLAG

The Guatemalan national flag has three equal vertical bands of light blue, white, and light blue. A coat of arms is imprinted on the white band. It consists of a green and red quetzal (the national bird) and a scroll superimposed on a pair of crossed rifles and crossed swords. All these symbols are framed by a wreath. The scroll bears the inscription LIBERTAD 15 DE SEPTIEMBRE DE 1821, Guatemala's original date of independence from Spain.

ECONOMY

GUATEMALA'S FREE-MARKET economy is based primarily on agriculture, with half the workforce employed on farms, ranches, and plantations. Agriculture accounts for almost one-quarter of the gross national product (GNP) and two-fifths of all exports. About one-third of the workforce is employed in services or tourism-related activities. Another 15 percent is engaged in manufacturing industries, such as food processing, pharmaceuticals, rubber, paper, and textiles.

The country's highlands and coastal plain yield the most productive soil. It is not surprising that most of the economically important farms and plantations are situated in these areas. Big corn-growing farms are found in the highlands, while the coastal plain is devoted mostly to coffee, sugarcane, and fruit cultivation. Very large cattle ranches are found closer to the Pacific coast. In the highlands, other than the big corn farms, most farms are small traditional homesteads that grow corn, beans, and squash for domestic consumption.

Guatemala City is the focus of nearly all industrial and commercial businesses in the country. One disadvantage of this, however, is that the capital suffers from pollution and congestion. Suitable housing is another problem. Thousands of unemployed Guatemalans flock to the city, hoping to find work. New shanty dwellings that spring up to accommodate them are often overcrowded and unsanitary.

Guatemala has become one of the world's major suppliers of cardamom—the fruit of an herb in the ginger family. There is also a small fishing industry centered along the Pacific Ocean coastline. Other small but developing industries deal in petroleum and the mining of antimony, iron ore, and lead. The oil industry is based mostly in Petén and poses a mortal threat to Petén's rain forests.

Above: **A young boy tends to a grocery store in Guatemala City.**

Opposite: **Dressed in their traditional handwoven garments, these women carry flowers to sell at a weekly outdoor market in Chichicastenango.**

After coffee, sugar is the nation's largest export commodity.

A major slice of Guatemala's income derives from its citizens who work abroad, especially in the United States. They remit an estimated $500 million annually.

EXPORTS AND IMPORTS

Coffee and sugar are Guatemala's most important exports, followed by bananas, cardamom, and cotton. The country is diversifying from its traditional reliance on coffee after prices plunged in 2001 and export earnings were drastically cut. There is also a substantial demand for its vegetables, fruit, and flowers. The main market for this produce is the United States—45 percent of such goods are sent there. Other important trading nations are China, El Salvador, and South Korea.

The United States is also the most significant import trading partner, accounting for more than 30 percent of imports. From the United States, Guatemala imports electrical machinery, metal equipment, and chemical products for use in its own industrial production. Textiles and food are also imported. Mexico provides essential supplies of petroleum. China and El Salvador are major business partners as well.

The country's main port is Santo Tomás de Castilla, which is situated on the Caribbean coast.

INDUSTRY

Industrial activity accounts for over 19 percent of Guatemala's GNP. Many small factories and industrial concerns are based in and around Guatemala City.

The main industrial activities are concentrated on food, tobacco, and sugar processing. There are also small industries involved in the manufacturing of textiles and clothing, tires, cement, and pharmaceuticals. The United States offers a ready market for most of these products. Petroleum refining is another promising business. Although it currently accounts for less than 5 percent of the GNP, it is an industry that has potential for development.

The service sector is a vital economic contributor. While it employs only about a third of the workforce, it generated almost 60 percent of the country's gross domestic product (GDP) in 2006. That is expected to grow even further as more tourists flock to Guatemala for its archaeological and geographical attractions. Official unemployment figures are quite low, standing at around 3.2 percent in 2005.

Timber is a valuable export resource but the industry is at odds with national efforts to preserve the rain forests.

A Guatemalan's per capita income, which is the average amount of money that he or she earns annually, is approximately US $5,000. In reality, however, this is not typical, as the wealth distribution is uneven and 56 percent of the population lives below the poverty line.

CARDAMOM

Cardamom is a spice that is the fruit of the herb *Elettaria cardamomum*, a member of the ginger family. In Guatemala the plants grow up to a height of 20 feet (6 m) and produce long, flowering shoots. The petals are greenish with a purplish white lip. The fruit is dried in the sun after picking and turns from a bright red to a dark brown color.

Aromatic cardamom seeds have a spicy flavor and are popularly used as a seasoning in curries and other spicy dishes. Most cardamom is likely to have come from Guatemala—the world's largest exporter of this spice. Large amounts of it are exported to the Persian Gulf states because of the popularity of cardamom-flavored coffee in countries such as Saudi Arabia.

The highlands of Alta Verapaz, about 62 miles (100 km) north of the capital, rely heavily on cardamom cultivation. The processed spice is vital to the local economy, as up to 200,000 people earn their living from this variety of agriculture. The first cardamom seeds were planted in the Alta Verapaz region. They were taken there from India by Germans who were, at the time, heavily involved in the coffee industry.

COFFEE—SMOKY AND SPICY

Guatemala produces more coffee than any other country in Central America. The coffee industry is prone to price fluctuations, however, and is dependent on favorable weather conditions. Guatemalan coffee is noted for its smoky, spicy flavor, which makes it one of the world's best-loved brews.

The lore of Guatemalan coffee dates back to the early years of Spanish rule when the Jesuits cultivated coffee trees as ornamental plants. In the

second half of the 19th century, rising world demand led to the rapid expansion of coffee plantations that were mostly run by German immigrants. Indians who were forced off their land to make way for plantations were subsequently made to labor on the same plantations. By 1914 German immigrants owned half the land that was being used for coffee production. As much as 50 percent of the country's total coffee yield was exported to Germany. Most of the Germans were expelled from Guatemala during World War II, but the coffee industrialists remain a powerful economic and political force today.

Coffee farming in Guatemala posed some problems for the early cultivators, but German immigrants evolved a process that protected coffee plants during periods of cold weather. Pitch was burned close to the rows of plants because the dense smoke helped keep the frost away from the plants and also imparted a smoky flavor to the coffee beans. The rich volcanic soil and ideal temperature enable the cultivation of several varieties of coffee beans in the country, with the highest quality beans growing at an altitude of around 5,000 feet (1,520 m).

Coffee beans ripening before the harvest season. Coffee is one of Guatemala's most important export products, prized for its high quality.

Once a mainstay of the economy, bananas are now part of a more diverse agricultural export industry.

Reliance on cash crops can be risky. In 1998 Hurricane Mitch destroyed 98 percent of Guatemala's banana crop, drastically reducing the country's export earnings.

A BANANA REPUBLIC

Some 30 miles (50 km) inland from the Caribbean coast, to the east of Lake Izabal, lies the small town of Bananera. As the name suggests, this is banana territory, producing the bulk of Guatemala's annual exports. The origin of the town's name goes back to the 19th century when the United Fruit Company—a U.S. company—chose the town as the headquarters of its banana-exporting business. At the time there was no proper infrastructure for transportation, so the company built its own railways and developed the port of Puerto Barrios. The demand for bananas in the United States was insatiable toward the end of the 19th century. By 1899, over 16 million bananas per year were being consumed in the United States, and they all came from Guatemala through the United Fruit Company.

In some respects the United Fruit Company was considered an enlightened employer, providing staff health care and housing. It also made massive profits because wages were low and company taxes were almost nonexistent. In time, the company's power grew to such an extent that it virtually had the entire Guatemalan economy in its grip. Evidence of its power and control became obvious in 1954. A reform government attempted to take over unused company land but was rebuffed and replaced by a new, unelected government that supported the company.

The United Fruit Company no longer exists, and its interests in Guatemala are now part of the Del Monte corporation. Large banana plantations still surround the town of Bananera, and exports of this valuable fruit continue to represent an important part of the country's economy.

TOURISM

In recent years, the money spent by tourists in Guatemala has become an important source of foreign exchange. In 1993 tourism had already become the second-largest revenue generator, after coffee. There were times when many potential visitors were turned off by outbreaks of violence and evidence of systematic human rights abuses. The signing of the Peace Accords in 1996 ushered in a period of growth and development. More than a decade later, Guatemala has welcomed over 1.3 million visitors, who poured an estimated $870 million into the economy of the country.

It is also possible that revenue gained through tourism will reach wider sections of the population than just the small elite that currently enjoys a disproportionate amount of the country's wealth. Tourists visiting

A tourist, using her cell phone to take a picture with a local woman at the famous Mayan ruins in Tikal.

A young tourist crouches by a pool of water at the Las Siete Altares waterfalls at Izabal.

The United Fruit Company acquired the nickname El Pulpo (ell PULL-poh), Spanish for octopus, because of the way it managed to exert its control and influence over the many different parts of the country's economy.

Guatemala are often more likely to spend their money among the people who operate market stalls or guided tours. This in turn means that the money is circulated among the lower levels of the domestic economy.

Many of the more popular destinations for visitors are in the Petén area, especially Tikal and Uaxactún. Enterprising Indian families who are able to offer accommodations or sell locally produced handicrafts are most likely to benefit from tourism.

The highlands, too, attract many visitors. They are drawn by the cultural integrity of the region's Indian society, its splendid Mayan ruins, and the exciting spectacle of the world's largest Indian market, in Chichicastenango. Antigua, the original capital, is popular because of its 18th-century colonial architecture and relaxed atmosphere. It was designated a UNESCO World Heritage Site in 1979. Lake Atitlán is one of the scenic areas in the country that remains a prime tourist attraction.

The tourism industry's growth, nevertheless, may endanger Guatemala's physical and cultural environment. Ecotourism offers the best hope for continuity, as it allows Guatemalans to benefit economically, at the same time preserving their cultural heritage.

ECOTOURISM

Ecotourism is based on the idea of sustainable travel. It is a way to encourage and benefit from tourism without inflicting irreversible damage on the host culture. This concept involves educating both the visitors and local people. Such a program has been successfully implemented in neighboring Belize and Costa Rica. For example, Petén's rain forest has tremendous short-term economic value as a source of timber. As the largest surviving tract of tropical woodlands in North and Central America, however, it also offers long-term value as an ecotourist destination. Local residents, with their knowledge of the flora and fauna, can be employed as guides. More visitors are opting for authentic accommodations provided by the local population. Both the making and wearing of traditional Indian dress has increased over recent years. This has partly been attributed to the growing commercial demand for cultural handicrafts.

Since the signing of the Peace Accords, tourism has grown dramatically. Influential Guatemalans hope that ecotourism will develop rapidly into a viable economic resource. The industry had a healthy start with the success of Tikal National Park—a protected area of 222 square miles (575 square km)—that houses spectacular ancient Mayan ruins.

ENVIRONMENT

GUATEMALA'S BEAUTY IS DAZZLING. Lavishly endowed by Mother Nature, the country's wealth of natural resources offers a welcome relief from its political, economic, and social turmoil. During the day snowcapped mountains and sky blue lakes beckon. At nightfall molten orange lava lights up the sky above smoldering volcanoes. Now and then sun-bleached Mayan cities rise above rolling stretches of emerald forests. Obviously, Guatemala is a canvas of radiant colors.

Sadly, these postcard-perfect landscapes are fading by the minute. An onslaught of threats, from deforestation to pollution and urbanization, is sapping the country's rich ecological legacy. Guatemala may be among the world's top 25 countries in terms of plant diversity, but environmental concerns invariably take a backseat when the majority of its people are struggling to survive.

Since the 1990s, the government, local partners, and international organizations have set up serious conservation efforts. There is growing public awareness about the importance of preserving Guatemala's natural treasures before they are lost for good.

Left: **Lake Atitlán with its three surrounding volcanoes is just one of the many breathtaking vistas found in Guatemala.**

Opposite: **An aerial view of the Motagua River juxtaposes the beauty of the different landforms against one another.**

This forest in Petén has been destroyed by a slash-and-burn type fire.

DEFORESTATION

Guatemala derives its name from the Aztec word Quauhtlemallan, which means "land of many trees." Forests and woodlands blanket 36 percent of the country. Sadly, human activities are threatening this rich natural heritage. Slash-and-burn agriculture, cattle ranching, logging, and land development have gutted vast tracts of forest greenery. Every year 2 percent of Guatemala's estimated 9.7 million acres (3.9 million ha) of forests are wiped out.

When trees are felled for crop cultivation or to make way for pastures, the limited vegetative cover that remains is not enough to protect the soil from intense rain and blazing sunshine. Overgrazing by livestock loosens the earth, which accelerates the process of soil erosion. Thunderstorms wash away layers of the topsoil into waterways where muddy sediments accumulate, thus crippling aquatic ecologies. Prolonged exposure to heat and moisture also results in laterization, a process that causes the soil to harden until it becomes bricklike and incapable of nourishing any plant or animal life.

Massive deforestation has scarred the landscape, replacing highland pine and oak forests with patches of savanna. The problem worsens when tropical rain forests are cleared. Besides regulating the climate, these deep jungles sustain an incredible array of wildlife within a limited area. When their fragile ecosystems are molested, rain forests take decades to regenerate and may never recover their original diversity. Over the last 60 years, rapid deforestation has stripped Central America of about 85 percent of its rain forest areas.

Naturalists fear that this is the situation in Petén. Dense foliage is cut down to make way for road networks, creating a suitable infrastructure for foreign companies to explore underground oil reserves. In this speculative process, Guatemala's 250 mammal species, 463 bird types, 342 reptile and amphibian species, as well as 8,681 plant varieties, all face habitat loss and possible extinction.

LOGGING

Commercial logging is another culprit that results in deforestation. Despite having laws governing forestry management, scofflaw organizations continue to plunder Guatemalan jungles. In 2005 Guatemala's timber production reached 21.8 million cubic yards (16.7 million cubic m).

Prized mahogany logs at a lumberyard, destined for export markets.

Trees are felled for fuel, furniture, and construction purposes. Tropical hardwoods such as mahogany and cedar are especially popular. Since the late 19th century, mahogany has been harvested in Petén. Mahogany is prized for its beautiful color and durability. Known to be one of the world's most expensive varieties of wood, a single mature tree that is sold for $50 can produce luxury furniture valued around $18,000 in European markets. Demand is even higher in North America, which imports about 60 percent of the world's mahogany.

Most of the mahogany that is sold worldwide is illegally harvested. Persistent high demand for wood has resulted in the extinction of many species. To combat this deadly pattern, Guatemala joined forces with Nicaragua to propose strict regulations on the Latin American mahogany trade. The Conference on International Trade in Endangered Species (CITES) approved their plan in 2002.

SLASH-AND-BURN FARMING

A traditional agricultural practice known as slash-and-burn is an intensive farming method. It can damage the land permanently.

The farmer usually clears a plot of land between 3 to 5 acres (1.2 to 2 ha) in size. This is the maximum area that his family is able to cultivate. All vegetation on the site is burned, so the resultant minerals that are released boost soil fertility temporarily. Crops such as corn and yams are planted for three to six years, after which the soil's nutrients are exhausted and productivity declines. The plot is then abandoned. The family chooses another area to prepare for subsistence cultivation, repeating the prodigal cycle.

Slash-and-burn farming was not as harmful to the environment in the past because the population was low and there was plenty of unclaimed land for cultivation. Besides, there was sufficient time for the used plots to lie fallow before they could be farmed again.

Population growth in recent times, however, exerts immense pressure on the terrain. Plots are intensely farmed and are not given enough time to restore their mineral nutrients. Heavy rainfall also causes the plots' mineral supply to be drained away more quickly, so new areas must be cleared to produce the same amount of crops. A deforested plot can be burned just twice before it becomes infertile, leaving a swath of barren landscape in its wake.

Slash-and-burn farming has remorselessly encroached on Guatemala's remaining rain forests. Besides menacing traditional lifestyles and cultures, it also imperils the very existence of the country's wildlife network.

ENDANGERED SPECIES

A variety of flora and fauna thrives within each of Guatemala's distinct geographic sectors. From the fertile Pacific coastal plains to fiery volcanic peaks, from misty cloud forests to rain-drenched tropical jungles, all are home to thousands of plants and an equally mind-boggling number of wildlife species. Many of these are endemic, or native, to the country and cannot be found anywhere else in the world.

The white nun orchid or *monja blanca* (MON-HA blan-KA) is extremely rare. As its name suggests, the blossom looks like a nun wearing traditional white robes. Unfortunately, it is in danger of extinction. Although it is Guatemala's national flower, the white nun orchid is seldom cultivated outside the Verapaz region. Found mainly at altitudes of 3,900 to 5,900 feet (1,200 to 1800 m) around the mountains of Cobán, the serene orchid symbolizes peace and beauty.

The quetzal is another Guatemalan national emblem that faces possible extermination. Dark green and brilliant red in color, this fruit-eating bird has a small body and spiky tufts on its head. The male quetzal is sought after for its flamboyant tail feathers, which are bright green and can grow to 24 inches (60 cm) long. The ancient Mayas and Aztecs revered Quetzalcoatl, the serpent god who was always depicted wearing an elaborate headdress made of quetzal feathers. The bird was such an important feature in their culture that anyone caught hunting the quetzal would be put to death!

Modern-day Guatemala still holds the quetzal in awe. The national currency is named after it. The indigenous people see it as an icon of

The exquisite Guatemalan national flower, the white nun orchid, faces the peril of becoming extinct.

Guatemala's national tree, the ceiba, is a tropical hardwood that is commonly found in Latin American rain forests.

51

freedom, as they believe that the quetzal dies of a broken heart when it is held in captivity. The reclusive bird is difficult to track down. Its migratory nature and inaccessible locales make quetzal sighting a scarce occurrence. Deforestation has also destroyed many of the mountainous forests that were its natural habitat.

WATER POLLUTION

While Guatemala's water resources are plentiful, their quality is a concern. Private corporations, power plants, municipalities, and even domestic households continue with their daily affairs and the freshwater, coastal, and marine bodies suffer. The country has defined a water policy to regulate the use of the resource to control the situation.

Studies have confirmed that forests affect the availability of ground and surface water in neighboring catchment areas. Land clearance, burning, or dredging increases soil erosion and siltation in water channels. When these sediments are carried into the sea, they disrupt the water clarity and retard coral growth. Sewage, harmful chemical effluents, and runoffs generated from industrial and agricultural activities cause eutrophication—a process in which there is increased plant growth and decay. Algae colonies proliferate, choking off the oxygen supply to marine organisms and eventually suffocating entire aquatic ecosystems. Conservationists are working to rescue reefs along the Polochic and Montague rivers from such a fate.

A male quetzal perching on a tree branch.

EXTINCTION THROUGH TOURISM

In the late 1950s, the black bass was introduced into Lake Atitlán in an attempt to spawn a sportfishing industry. The black bass is a voracious feeder, and one of its hapless victims was the Atitlán grebe—a small waterbird whose inability to fly made it particularly vulnerable to its predators. By the mid-1960s, fewer than a hundred grebes survived. Their numbers continued to fall as growing tourist development disturbed their natural habitat. Found nowhere else in the world, the Atitlán grebe is now extinct.

Years of environmental mismanagement have also defiled formerly scenic landscapes. To the south of Guatemala City lies Lake Amatitlán where the once clear waters are now contaminated. It used to be a popular picnic place for the capital's residents.

A large number of Guatemalans lack access to proper waste-disposal facilities. Household refuse is often dumped in open drainage channels. Industrial garbage, including sludge deposits from oil extractions and mining wastes, pollutes waterways. Such biological and chemical contamination has fouled water quality in many reservoirs, making it impossible to enjoy such recreational pursuits as boating.

Another consequence of serious water pollution is the prevalence of waterborne diseases. Guatemala tops the charts in this issue. The country's

The Mayas perfected the art of trapping the quetzal alive and removing its prized tail feathers before releasing it back into the wild so that the bird might grow its splendid plumage all over again.

The heavily polluted waters curtail recreational activities at Lake Amatitlán.

Guatamalans are making efforts to clean up the garbage and jetsam from the estuary of the Villalobo River, which flows into the now very polluted Lake Amatitlán.

general lack of potable water, inadequate sewerage systems, and deficient solid waste disposal facilities have resulted in the spread of diseases such as cholera, typhoid, dysentery, and hepatitis. Guatemala registered the highest cholera infection rate in Central America when, in 1995, 707 out of every 100,000 people were infected.

PROTECTED AREAS

The country's astonishing biodiversity is clearly of enormous value for the conservation movement and research. The National Council of Protected Areas (CONAP) works with nature groups such as Fundación Defensores de la Naturaleza (the World Wildlife Fund's Guatemalan partner), Vivamos Mejor (Let's Live Better), and international organizations in managing national protected areas. Presently, parks and nature reserves make up over 15 percent of Guatemala.

Next to the Amazon, the Maya Biosphere is the second largest tropical forest ecosystem in Latin America. The Guatemalan section, stretching from

Mexico to Belize, is concentrated in Petén and encompasses over 9,374 square miles (24,280 square km)—an area almost triple the size of Yellowstone National Park. It consists mainly of tropical rain forests. Parts of the reserve are managed according to the Forestry Stewardship Council policy for sustainable logging. The Maya Biosphere is also home to Tikal National Park, a UNESCO World Heritage Site, and Mario Dary Rivera Park, which is dedicated to the preservation of the quetzal.

The Sierra de las Minas Biosphere Reserve is another treasured national park. The oldest mountain range in Central America is also one of its most spectacular. Towering at 9,843 feet (3,000 m), the peaks pierce the sky. The rugged terrain sustains two-thirds of Guatemala's and Belize's total mammal species. Besides offering a safe haven for endangered jaguars, tapirs, howler monkeys, scarlet macaws, and harpy eagles, the reserve is also a vital "gene bank" for many coniferous evergreen trees and shrubs.

Other notable sites include the Balam Ku State Reserve—famed for its immense bat cave—and the Chocón Machacas reservation near Livingston, which was set up to protect the manatee and the mangrove swamps dotting the Caribbean coast.

As is the case in many developing nations, managing protected areas is a year-round challenge. Resources are limited, and funds are heavily dependent on the prevailing sociopolitical climate. During Guatemala's 36-year civil war, much-needed finances were often channeled to military expenses instead. Environmental preservation is hampered further by a lack of equipment and skilled personnel.

Visitors leisurely walking in the Quirigua National Archaeological Park.

THE MAYA BIOSPHERE RESERVE

Established in 1990, the Maya Biosphere Reserve (MBR) is a joint conservation effort of the government and UNESCO (United Nations Educational, Scientific, and Cultural Organization). Set up to promote a balanced relationship between humans and ecosystems, the MBR is Guatemala's largest protected area, occupying over 13 percent of the nation's total territory.

This sprawling expanse of forested canopy is the bastion for lush biota—the region's flora and fauna. It embraces different life zones, including flat wetlands and humid tropical jungles. As part of the International Network of Biosphere Reserves, this environment nurtures over 95 mammal species, 45 reptile species, 18 amphibian species, 112 fish species, 400 bird species, and over 375 different types of plants.

The Maya Biosphere is divided into three zones, each with a distinct land use. Most forms of development are prohibited in the legally protected core area, which covers 5.1 million acres (2.1 million ha). This wilderness zone has been set aside solely for nature conservation. Another 2.1 million acres (850,000 ha) are designated for multiple use. Bordering the core area, this sector promotes better management of forestry resources. Here, the indigenous Indians practice sustainable agriculture such as environmentally responsible logging, harvest allspice, and cultivate xate fern—a tropical palm that is commonly used in floral arrangements. Finally, a surrounding buffer zone of 1.2 million acres (486,000 ha) is set aside for private holdings. Small-plot farmers and park workers customarily live there.

The reserve is arguably best known for Tikal National Park. The 140,000-acre (57,000 ha) World Heritage Site was formerly the cradle of the ancient Maya empire, one of the world's most advanced civilizations whose people mysteriously abandoned their power base around the year 900. The Smithsonian Institution estimates that 15 percent of tourists who visit Guatemala are drawn to Tikal National Park's natural and archaeological splendors.

CONSERVATION EFFORTS / PROGRAMS

Guatemala has endorsed international treaties on biodiversity, climate change, endangered species, and wetlands conservation.

Various stakeholders, such as landowners, nature groups, private institutions, government officials, and scientists, play crucial roles in preserving fragile ecosystems. Besides protecting precious species, successful conservation efforts also seek to educate local communities so that they benefit from such measures.

Guatemala's Decree 5-90 governing land use is one example of field conservation, wherein land is set aside for the cultivation of nontimber products. People are encouraged to harvest renewable forest resources such as chicle (used in chewing gum) and allspice for income. A family can daily earn three times more from harvesting such products than from clearing forest, planting corn, and raising cattle.

In the first public-private agreement of its kind in Latin America, the World Wildlife Fund collaborated with the Guatemalan government to maintain Sierra del Lacandón National Park. Both parties also created the area's first five-year master plan. In 2006 the international organization Nature Conservancy helped Fundación Defensores de la Naturaleza purchase almost 100,000 acres (41,000 ha) of privately owned land in Sierra del Lancandón, thus safeguarding pristine forests and a crucial Mayan ruin.

Debt-for-nature swaps are another form of conservation. In 2006 the United States wrote off several million dollars of Guatemalan debt on condition that the nation use that amount to finance forest conservation within its borders. The treaty requires Guatemala to make regular debt payments to a Conservation Trust Fund. Organizations such as Nature Conservancy and Conservation International will each contribute $1 million while the U.S. government will forgive $15 million in debt. Those amounts and the interests they generate are expected to eventually cancel the $24.4 million that Guatemala owes the United States.

The Guatemalan deal was the largest reached since the Tropical Forest Conservation Act was ratified. Over the next 15 years, the trust fund will distribute grants to local NGOs (nongovernmental organizations) that work to protect crucial habitats in the Maya, Sierra de Las Minas, and Sierra Madre Biospheres.

Tikal National Park is now a protected zone. More and more forested areas are currently also being preserved, in a bid to protect Guatemala's incredibly diverse ecosystems.

GUATEMALANS

THERE ARE OVER 12 million people living in Guatemala, mostly either Indians or Ladinos. Indians constitute just under half of the population, making Guatemala one of the few countries in the world where there is a significant American Indian presence. Portraits of ancient Maya people inscribed in stone bear the same facial characteristics as contemporary Indians. When the Spanish arrived in 1523, Indians populated the entire country, but European diseases wiped out a large proportion of the indigenous population. In some regions over 75 percent of the inhabitants died. It was not until the end of the 17th century that the Indian population regained its pre-Columbian level. By then high intermixing rates between those of Spanish heritage and the Indians had produced a new category of people, known as Ladinos.

Today Ladinos account for 59 percent of the population. They wear Western-style clothing, generally enjoy a higher standard of living than the Indians, and tend to dominate in positions of authority and influence in the country. Nearly all the larger commercial establishments and all the large tracts of privately owned land belong to Ladinos. The 1996 Peace Accords provided an opportunity to redress the social and political inequality between the two peoples. In 1997 Rigoberta Menchú, the award-winning activist Indian writer, was offered a ministerial post in the government as part of that process. A decade later, she ran for the presidency.

Some 41 percent of the population is under 15 years of age, 4 percent are senior citizens over the age of 65, and the remaining population, between 15 and 64 years, makes up just over half the population. The population has an annual growth rate of 2.1 percent.

Above: **Local girls in their school uniforms. Unlike their rural counterparts, many urban Guatemalans have a very westernized sense of style.**

Opposite: **A young girl wearing a colorful print shirt carries a load of produce on her head in the village of Sololá.**

Guatemala's Indians are the direct descendants of the gifted Maya people who were able to plot the course of Venus and build complex pyramid temples over a thousand years ago.

INDIANS

Maya Indians are spread across Central America. While the majority are concentrated in Guatemala, some reside in southern Mexico, Honduras, and Belize. Seven out of every eight Indians in Central and South America could trace their roots to Guatemala. Around 1900 about 80 percent of the country's population was Maya, but it has now dropped to about 40 percent. The exact figure remains disputed because of undercounting during the country's 2001 official census.

There are different groups within Central America's Indian population. In Guatemala, the Mam people inhabit the northwest highlands, the Quiché are mainly clustered in the midwestern highlands, and the eastern highlands are home to the Pokomam. These three are the largest Mayan groupings, and each is divided into smaller tribes, each with its own distinct language. The Quiché group includes the Cakchiquel, and the Pokomam clan includes the Kekchí. Another major group, the Tzutujil, resides in the southwestern highlands.

Most of the Indians of modern Guatemala share certain physical characteristics. They tend to be short but stocky, with straight black hair, dark eyes, and skin color that varies from copper to brown. They are also likely to have a broad face, high cheekbones, and a low forehead.

INDIAN FEMALE DRESS

Exotic colors are characteristic of the traditional Indian dress that helped Guatemala win the title for best native costume in the Miss Universe pageant of 1967, starting the fashion interest in the vibrant hues that make American or European clothes seem dull and unimaginative. Women's clothing has managed to retain greater continuity with the Mayan past than male attire.

There are about 150 villages in Guatemala where local women still regularly wear traditional Indian dress featuring designs and colored patterns unique to their particular village.

Popular names for Guatemalan boys include Mateo, Juan, Carlos, Edwin, Roberto, and Miguel. Popular girls' names are Maria, Lucrecia, and Ana. Almost everyone has a second name and typical examples are Ana Maria and Miguel Angel.

The *huipil* (WEE-pil) commands the most importance among traditional outfits. A roomy sleeveless tunic or overblouse that was once worn loose, it is now tucked into a wraparound or gathered skirt. Women often add a touch of individuality to their skirts by sewing on colored strips of embroidered cloth, known as *randa* (RAND-ah). There are also traditional capes or shawls worn around the shoulders and various waist sashes. Blouses are commonly worn, although these are a legacy of the Spanish culture.

What distinguishes all these items of dress is not so much the basic design but, rather, their sophisticated and colorful embroidery. Pictorial themes based on indigenous mythical or magical flora and fauna are very popular. Many of the patterns are believed to have descended directly from ancient Mayan culture. In recent years, following the success of literacy campaigns, *huipils* have also been embroidered with the name of the wearer's village. The more intricately decorated *huipils* take months to make, especially when the fabric is woven in a complicated pattern, using a backstrap loom. Women sometimes wear their best *huipils* inside out so as to lengthen the embroidery's lifespan. Many will wear their garment only for a special outing, such as market day or a fiesta.

A mother braids her daughter's hair. Traditional embroidery patterns identify the area the wearer comes from. For Indians, traditional dress is an important link to their culture and heritage.

Different communities have their own customary patterns, and it is easy to identify a woman's home village from her attire. For example, women from Santiago Atitlán, near Lake Atitlán, wear *huipils* that are adorned with white and purple stripes. They also wear the *tocayal* (toe-CAY-al)—a bright red head wrap—which is depicted on one of the country's coins. Some head wraps have tassels or pom-poms.

The town of Nahualá is represented by a twin-headed eagle, which is thought to be a remnant of the symbolic regalia of the Hapsburg family that ruled Spain when Guatemala was colonized.

INDIAN MALE DRESS

Indian male clothing displays more Spanish influence, but traditional touches are also evident. The town of Sololá and the surrounding highlands are famous for their traditional Indian clothing. When British writer Aldous Huxley visited the Sololá market in the 1930s, he described it as "a walking museum of fancy dress."

The traditional Indian male attire includes short baggy trousers that are embroidered in the same style as their jackets. Colorful cowboy shirts complete the outfits. Jackets are often plain, in simple black and white with frogging—ornamental cording for fastening clothing. An emblematic bat is usually added on the back. The bat was the symbol of the ruling Mayan royal family before the Spanish arrived.

Rodilleras (row-dee-YEH-raz) and *ponchitos* (pon-CHEE-tos) are woolen blankets, usually woven on a foot-treadled loom (instead of the common backstrap loom), which men

A man carrying a load on his back. Outside the larger cities, some Indian men continue to dress in their traditional styles.

wear over their trousers. *Ponchito* is the name for the shorter version, and there are some interesting regional differences in the way it is worn. Sololá residents drape it around the hips with a belt and a folded-over section at the top that covers the belt. In other areas, the *ponchito* is a lot smaller and is only worn in front like an apron. Sometimes the *ponchito* is embroidered with a colorful band at each end and has a white border.

Men commonly wear hats that come in a variety of sizes and materials such as straw, wool, or even palm leaf. More expensive leather hats are reserved for special occasions.

Many men, even when decked out in Western pants and a dress shirt, carry a small traditional shoulder bag made from wool.

THE PLIGHT OF INDIANS

The Indians' suffering began with the Spanish conquest, when the conquistadors were given land rights as rewards for their services. In addition to land, the Spanish were entitled to demand native labor without pay and could also tax workers through enforced contributions of goods such as cloth and salt.

There were five Indian revolts in the 18th century and seven in the 19th century, every one of which was brutally suppressed. Long after the official abolition of slavery, the Maya continued to be treated as slaves. Even in the 19th century, it was common to find peasants who were forced to work for their landowners as a means of repaying a "loan." In reality, loans could never be repaid and the peasants remained virtual slaves.

In the 1930s laws were passed obliging Indians to work on plantations. The socialist governments in power from 1945 to 1954 acknowledged the plight of these Indians. Nonetheless, this empty gesture did very little to put an end to their suffering.

Things did not improve following the U.S.-sponsored military coup in 1954. Successive military governments treated the Indians in much the

An Indian woman showing a portrait of her husband who was a victim of the civil war. The government has actively started to compensate the relatives of war victims. An estimated 200,000 people, mostly Mayan Indian civilians, were killed during the country's 36-year civil war.

same way the Spanish had. Indigenous people were the chief victims of the military's systematic abuse of human rights in recent decades, partly because they were the ones that various guerrilla movements turned to for support. Many Guatemalans hoped that the 1996 Peace Accords would lead to significant improvements for the Indians and their culture.

HEADDRESSES AND SANDALS

The stone carvings of the ancient Maya include images of interesting attire. Although contemporary Guatemalans no longer deck themselves in headdresses made of quetzal feathers as the Maya did, Indian women still like elaborate and visually arresting headgear.

Santiago Atitlán's women are particularly renowned for their headdresses, which are made from strips of colored cloth over 30 feet (9 m) in length. The cloth is continuously coiled around the head to form an impressive halo. The women of Aguacatán, also in the western highlands, are equally famous for their turbans that are made from multicolored pieces of cloth.

Some ancient carvings depicted high-backed sandals. In some parts of Guatemala today, men and women alike wear sandals that look very similar to those worn by their ancestors. The ancient Maya, however, never used the kind of sandals worn by poorer people today, which are cut out from discarded tires and tied together with thongs.

LADINOS

Ladinos, who make up more than half of Guatemala's population, are usually described as people of mixed Spanish and Indian blood. Sometimes, though, the term is not used in a racial sense. It can also be used to describe an Indian who has forsaken traditional dress and customs in favor of a Spanish lifestyle. Across Central America the general term for people of mixed Spanish and Indian blood is mestizo. Only in Guatemala are they known as Ladino. The term itself is Spanish and denotes one of the 16 racial castes that formed the population under Spanish colonial law.

Ladinos speak Spanish, and they tend not to acknowledge their obvious kinship with Mayan Indians, some even going so far as to claim that their ancestors were not Maya but Aztec or Toltec—Indians who came to Guatemala from Mexico and intermarried with the Spanish. It is more likely that Spanish soldiers, most of whom were not allowed to take their wives with them, took up with Indian women. In some cases they

Of mixed Spanish and Indian blood, these young Ladinos are the friendly face of modern urban Guatemala.

"For me, my traje *(TRAH-bay, traditional dress) is like a flag. It is not mine . . . rather, it belongs to a whole people. It contains so much, even mystical and spiritual value."*

—Words of a Maya Indian woman

would have been Mayan Indians, but because the Maya were reluctant to marry outside of their own racial group, commingling would also have included Indians from other parts of Central America.

Ladino culture is centered around Guatemala City for historical reasons. The capital was the seat of Spanish power, and it was also where Indians interacted with the Spanish. Today most Ladinos live in towns and cities across the western highlands, where they make up three-quarters of the population. They tend to dominate the commerce and politics of their localities. While most Indians are farmers, Ladinos are more likely to work in shops and government departments or as paid laborers in industries.

MINORITY GROUPS

The Garifuna—also known as Black Caribs—are members of a minority group that lives around Livingston on the Caribbean coast. The town has a small population of 3,000 and is the only place in Guatemala where a Garifuna community is found.

These people have a highly unusual history that goes back several centuries. Caribbean Indians and African slaves who were exiled from British colonies in the Caribbean made the Caribbean island of St. Vincent their home. In the 17th century, their descendants migrated to Central America. The Garifuna culture combines traditional Indian beliefs with elements of African heritage, but today their African ethnicity and cultural distinctiveness are gradually being diluted to the point of total absorption.

Many foreigners come to Guatemala to improve their Spanish. Antigua is well known for its language schools.

Some 3 percent of Guatemala's population come from the United States and Europe, Germany in particular. Their economic importance is far greater than what their small number suggests, as many of them are powerful industrialists or owners of large ranches. For a long time, the U.S.-based United Fruit Company accounted for a small but very powerful group of American expatriates, but that is no longer true as the company is now defunct. Some of the Germans living in Guatemala can trace their families back to the late 19th century when President Rufino Barrios sold land to German farmers to grow coffee. Non-Guatemalan white people are generally referred to as gringos. Gringo is often used to refer to a citizen of the United States, since most visitors come from there.

REFUGEES

During the 1970s and early 1980s, widespread persecution against the Indians led to thousands fleeing Guatemala for safer havens in Mexico and other countries. The new climate of peace has seen about 25,000 refugees returning to their country. Another 40,000 refugees live in United Nations–run camps in Mexico. Additionally, countless numbers of Guatemalans are living illegally in Mexico and the United States. Many are now considering returning to their homeland. A new government amnesty has also brought about the emergence of large groups of refugees who had remained in hiding in the country's remote corners. Over the next few years, all of them will be seeking reintegration and the start of a new life in Guatemalan society.

Many of the refugees face grievous housing problems. The shantytowns of Guatemala City can offer only a life of unemployed poverty, thus growing numbers are choosing to dwell in the underpopulated lowlands of Petén. This move causes far-reaching problems of yet another kind, as their slash-and-burn method of agriculture depletes the rain forest of valuable resources and affects whole populations of wildlife.

LIFESTYLE

THERE ARE TWO basic lifestyles in Guatemala—the urban Ladino culture and the mostly rural Indian existence. Wealth is so unevenly distributed that a Mayan family can expect to earn only half as much as a Ladino family. More Indian males than females move to urban areas and coastal plantations looking for work. Once the men are away from their own community, Ladino values tend to affect their lifestyle. Sociologists refer to this tendency as a process of "ladinization."

The Ladino lifestyle is recognizably Western, not just in terms of attire but also in regard to values and a generally materialistic attitude. Mayan customs do not dismiss the

Above: **Signs of popular shops in Guatemala's business district. Guatemalans residing in the city enjoy a very westernized way of life.**

Opposite: **Local women doing their washing beside the lake in Sololá. In rural parts, communal laundry areas are still used. They provide an important point of social contact, as well as a place to wash clothes.**

benefits of consumer goods and appliances, but such acquisitions are usually seen in terms of gaining status within the community, where the notions of honor and honesty are still held important. Indians rarely marry outside their community. The basic difference between the Ladino and Indian cultures dates back to the Spanish colonial rule. The Spanish regarded the Indians as ignorant pagans, a racist legacy that has, unfortunately, endured in modern-day Guatemala.

Traditionally, Mayan women have played an important role in ensuring the survival of Indian culture. Even when they are exposed to Ladino values while working as live-in maids or assembly-line employees in Guatemala City, they still tend to hold on to their customary traditional way of life. Many continue speaking their tribal languages and wearing traditional clothing. In the highlands, it is often the women who support the family by making and selling folk arts-and-crafts items. Booming demand for Mayan handicrafts has enabled artists—many of whom are females—to earn a living and enjoy economic security. This has also led to some changes in the traditional gender roles.

A boy looking listlessly at his surroundings. Poverty remains a problem in Guatemala. These rural dwellings are usually constructed and furnished with whatever the individual can find nearby. In the cities, too, shantytowns are common, and the lack of hygienic conditions poses health risks to many in the population.

POVERTY

Most Guatemalans are poor. Almost 56 percent of the population lives below the poverty line, and 16 percent survive in conditions of extreme poverty. This means that almost 2 out of every 10 Guatemalans subsist on less than $2 a day. Many of them stay in rural areas or the capital's slums, in ramshackle shanties made of wood, cardboard, or zinc sheets. They lack basic sanitation facilities and access to clean drinking water. The poorest residents cluster near dump sites and scavenge for recyclable items that they sell for meager earnings.

Skewed income distribution and blatant economic inequalities have caused much social tension. Money and power are concentrated in the hands of a small group of elites. According to 2002 figures, the richest 10 percent of Guatemalans control over 43 percent of the country's wealth. They enjoy an affluent lifestyle that is completely inaccessible, not just to the vast majority of the population but also to most people living in the capital. Every week hundreds of poverty-stricken peasants arrive in Guatemala City hoping for work. Rambling shantytowns continue to mushroom around the city outskirts. The more affluent Ladino residents tend to resent this intrusion, so poor Indians find themselves further disadvantaged when it comes to finding employment.

HEALTH

Health-care standards in Guatemala are generally poor, and statistics indicate the existence of serious health problems. The average life expectancy is about 68 years for men and 72 years for women, with Ladinos usually living longer than the indigenous people. This imbalance is partly caused by an uneven access to medical facilities. Many Indians reside in rural regions, with limited access to modern health care. The country's hospitals, doctors, and nurses are concentrated in Guatemala City, but only about 20 percent of the population lives in the capital. Inadequate facilities and insufficient medical personnel have contributed to the high infant mortality rate—the World Bank estimated that three in every 100 children die before the age of 3. Maternal mortality, or the number of mothers who die during childbirth, is the third highest among all Latin American countries. Aspects of health care that are taken for granted in the United States—inoculation against measles, for example—are sadly unavailable for the majority of Guatemalans.

Because of their inadequate diet, the rural poor suffer from malnutrition. Pregnant mothers who lack proper meals give birth to underweight babies that are especially vulnerable to illnesses. The main causes of infant mortality are diarrhea, respiratory infections, and childbirth problems, all of which might easily be prevented or attended to with the proper medical aid. Indeed, malnutrition is so widespread that many Guatemalan children experience stunted growth. Some 44 percent of them below five years are short for their age.

A malnourished child in Guatemala. Poverty has caused many children to suffer ill health.

RURAL LIFE

Well over half of the population lives in rural areas but the land is not fully utilized. Large landowners seldom use all their land and large tracts remain unexploited. The land that is farmed by an Indian family may be

MIGRATING FOR WORK

Migration is a fact of life in Guatemala. Countless families, Indian and Ladino alike, have been affected. The children of wealthy provincial families relocate to large cities seeking greener pastures or a more modern lifestyle. The need for work has forced poorer people to leave their homes in search of employment in urban areas. More Ladinos than Indians migrate to Guatemala City, although Indian migration from the highlands to the coastal plantations is very common.

Mayan laborers often take their young sons to the plantations, where they pick coffee beans to help supplement the family income. Mayan girls are commonly sent away to work as domestic servants in Ladino households. Such migration is often enacted on a seasonal basis, with the Indians returning to their villages and farms at important times such as during the planting and harvesting of corn.

More than half of the Guatemalan workforce is employed in agriculture, but fewer than 2 percent of landowners own over 65 percent of the land.

hours away from their home and situated high up the side of a mountain or on the slopes of a volcano. Typical rural villages suffer from serious underdevelopment. An obvious sign of this is the lack of a proper transportation system. Most roads that link villages in the countryside are unpaved and not maintained, so fallen rocks and broken stones may impede travel to the extent that a horse rider is able to travel almost as fast as the driver of a four-wheeled vehicle. Many remote villages have no connecting roads that can be used for travel by cars or carts. Not until 1970 was the first road built linking northern Petén with the rest of the country.

Most villages now have electricity, but some families cannot afford it. Even bottled gas is too expensive for many families, so they collect firewood as fuel for cooking and for keeping themselves warm at night. Most homes have no running water or toilets. Women collect water from a communal standpipe and carry it home in large containers balanced on their heads. Laundry is done at communal washing places or on the banks of a local river.

Traditionally the farming of corn is men's work. Women can inherit land and usually manage secondary crops such as beans and vegetables or tend to the family's livestock.

Cash crops like chilies and fruit are cultivated whenever possible and sold at the weekly village market. Chickens, turkeys, or pigs that are commonly found on an Indian farm are also sold at the market, but are rarely slaughtered for the table. Occasionally a chicken is cooked to provide a family feast during a local festival.

Children as young as 7 or 8 sometimes work alongside their parents on the family land and function productively as part of the household. The skills needed to make a living from the land are passed on from one generation to the next. In present times, however, it is common for young adults to leave their ancestral land to seek work opportunities in the cities.

FARMING CORN

Most Mayan Indians are subsistence farmers, and their plots of land are an important mark of their identity. Beans and corn are cultivated on these tracts. The Mayan attitude to land is influenced by their religious beliefs, which stress the vital economic importance of corn.

Corn seeds are planted in furrows, and when they sprout, the farmer protects them with a small mound of earth. It is common to plant other crops, such as beans and chili peppers, in the same *milpa* (MIL-pa), or field of corn. In the highlands, the farmer's cottage is often set in the middle of the *milpa*, an ancient practice that goes back into the time of the earliest Mayan communities.

In the lowlands, finding a regular supply of water cannot be taken for granted. When it does rain, depressions in the land become swampy, but these *bajos* (BAA-hos) can dry out completely. Farmers in the lowlands practice a slash-and-burn system of agriculture, which involves cutting

Father and son work the land with the help of cattle. Plowing the ash back into the ground after burning the forest to clear land adds valuable nutrients to the soil temporarily, but in the long run the deforestation causes barren earth.

An Indian farmer's plot of land is called a milpa, *and it forms an important part of one's heritage. Being a* milpero *(mill-PEAR-o), or small farmer, is an essential aspect of identifying oneself as a Maya.*

73

down a section of forest when it becomes dry toward the end of the year and setting it on fire. Small holes are made in the ash that the fire leaves behind and the corn kernels are then planted in them. This can be repeated the following year, but after that second cycle the ash-enriched soil is depleted of nutrients and a new section of the forest must be burned in order to repeat the process. Even in the highlands, the fields cannot be used indefinitely—there comes a time when the exhausted soil must be left fallow for a number of years to replenish its minerals. A farmer needs experience and skill to know when and where to farm. Slash-and-burn agriculture remains one of the main factors in the rapid destruction of the country's rain forests.

INDIAN HOMES

Traditional Indian homes are remarkably similar in design to those of the ancient Maya. The roof is usually thatched, or sometimes tiled, and the walls are made of adobe bricks or cornstalks. Walls are sometimes covered with a lime-based plaster. Only the more affluent villagers can afford to build a home with concrete blocks or use corrugated iron as a roof for their houses. There are usually no windows, and the earthen floors are covered with mats made from rushes, reeds, or palm leaves. The kitchen area consists of a humble fireplace made of stones set slightly apart in one corner of the room to keep the smoke away from the living quarters. Chimneys are not built; the smoke finds its own escape through the roof tiles or eaves. The *temaxcal* (tem-ASS-cal), a traditional steam bath dating back to pre-Columbian times, can sometimes be found a short distance apart from the home.

A subsistence farmer carefully tends his corn crop. Corn is the staple food crop of the Guatemalan people.

Domestic practices such as the making of sandals from animal hides and vegetable fibers still continue in present times. Although machines for grinding corn are becoming more common, many women still use stone tools for this age-old task.

Nearly every home has some kind of religious shrine. This is often in the form of a statue or a painting of a saint set on a small ledge or table decorated with colored cloth and candles. The sacrifice of animals to honor the gods, which extended to human sacrifices in ancient Mayan times, is still practiced among the Quiché Indians.

HUMAN RIGHTS

Guatemala has one of the poorest human rights records in all Latin America. Between the 1960s and the 1990s about 80,000 Guatemalans are estimated to have died at the hands of paramilitary death squads. Armed guerrillas fighting to overthrow the government represent only a fraction of this figure. Most of the victims were innocent civilians, largely Indians, whose villages were attacked because they allegedly were used as hiding places for guerrillas.

If someone were suspected of being politically opposed to the government, their family was likely to "disappear." The most graphic account of such human rights abuse is described in Rigoberta Menchú's

75

A bride kissing her groom outside an elaborately adorned church.

book *I, Rigoberta Menchú*. Trade union leaders and academics who were critical of government policies were frequently murdered. Even though the long years of fighting are finally over, critics of the government remain cautious of what they say. A U.S. government survey reported in 1996 that there was significant improvement in the general human rights situation but confirmed that problems still persist in many areas.

One area that has seen some improvement is the attention to the plight of street children in Guatemala City. Thousands of children with no families or homes roam the streets of the capital, leading lives of petty crime. On numerous occasions small groups of these children have been kidnapped and killed by unidentified men who are believed to have connections with the police.

MACHISMO AND MARRIAGE

Machismo, from the word "macho" (originally Spanish), or male, means a strong display of masculinity. The concept remains a recognizable aspect of cultural life across Central America. It is not frowned upon or ridiculed, simply because equality between the sexes is not taken for granted. A man's traditional role is that of head of the family—he literally builds the home—and a woman's role is that of supportive mother and homemaker.

Guatemalans tend to marry when they are fairly young, between the ages of 16 and 19. It is rare for Ladinos or Indians to marry outside their own communities.

INDIAN MARKET DAYS

Every village normally has one market day each week. Besides serving economic needs, the weekly market has a broad social significance. People come from surrounding areas to shop, sell surplus food or homemade crafts, meet friends, report news, and exchange gossip. Sometimes a party atmosphere develops the night before market day, with animated groups of people drinking to the sound of marimba music. Unless a bus service is available, Indians will often spend hours traveling on foot across mountain trails to their nearest village market, as many cannot afford to hire a mule to ride or to carry their goods. Whatever is taken to or purchased at the market has to be brought back home, so it is common to see Indian men traveling with a wooden crate slung from a leather band tied around the forehead. Women carry goods in baskets that are balanced on top of their heads.

A typical market day in an Indian village displays elements from both the traditional past and modern-day commercial cultures. Goods such as sandals, woven baskets, and hammocks are sold alongside canned food, inexpensive perfume, and costume jewelry of varying quality.

Handcrafted goods form an essential part of the village economy. Mats are in demand in every home, so there is always need for these, as well as for baskets. The latter are made either without handles—Indian women balance their baskets on their heads—or with handles for the Ladinos. Other common items that are sold in village markets are bags and nets made from fibers pulled from the agave plant. Pottery, in the form of plates, bowls, and cooking pots, are common handicraft items. These are shaped without using a potter's wheel and then are fired in the open.

Different Indian regions have their own traditional practices concerning the choice of a marriage partner. Some fathers with a son of marriageable age will employ a go-between to find a suitable daughter-in-law. Tradition requires the intended groom's parents to make a formal request to the parents of the intended bride. Parental approval is expected before an engagement is confirmed. When confirmed, an ox may be slaughtered to celebrate the event. Another feast follows the marriage ceremony itself, and the festivities may last for many days. The groom's family is expected to bear the cost of this feast as well as other wedding expenses.

CHEWING GUM, ARMADILLOS, AND MACAWS

In Petén, Indians supplement their meager incomes by harvesting latex from sapodilla trees. When ripe, the sweet sapodilla fruit is eaten, but the immature fruit is very hard and astringent. The bark of the tree contains chicle—a milky latex that is used to make chewing gum. The Indians work their way down from the top of these 65-foot- (20-m-) high trees, tapping into the bark with their machetes. The sap is collected at the bottom of the trees, dried, and then sold.

Another source of income is the armadillo. Relatively common in the Petén rain forest, armadillos are hunted for food and sold to restaurants or cooked at home. The brilliantly colored *guacamaya*, or scarlet macaw, is an endangered bird that is also hunted, as its flesh is in high demand.

According to custom, the newlywed couple will live with the groom's parents. In rural areas, it is common for the bride's family to receive some small gift from the groom's family as a symbolic "exchange" for the daughter. Divorce is very unusual. In the past, if the marriage did not work out, the bride price would be returned and the relationship dissolved.

Traditionally, the marriage ceremony would always take place in the presence of the village shaman, or high priest, but nowadays many young people have either a civil or church ceremony, or they may choose to dispense with a ceremony altogether. No matter which type of observation takes place, wedding rings are rarely exchanged.

EDUCATION

Education is compulsory for Guatemalan children age 7 to 12. Students are expected to attend six years of primary school followed by six years of secondary education. Secondary students usually have to complete three years of general or basic studies and three years of diversified studies. The last three years of secondary education are spent preparing for examinations that may lead to university entry or to other institutions of higher learning.

In reality, education is not available to everyone. Fewer than half the children attend elementary school, and, unfortunately, many drop out halfway. A World Bank report in 2004 estimated that Guatemalan children attend school for an average of only 4.3 years. As a result, the national illiteracy rate is very high. Between 31 to 45 percent of the adult population cannot read or write, which means Guatemala has the third-highest illiteracy rate in Latin America.

Among the Indian population, the illiteracy rate is even higher. This is especially the case for females, with 62 percent of Indian women being uneducated. One reason for this is that many parents need their children to work on the farms, so resist sending them to school. Another reason is the language barrier. Classes are usually taught in Spanish, which poses a major barrier for Indian children who speak only their native languages.

In recent years, Indians have successfully set up their own schools using their own languages. Formally recognized by the government in 1988, the Academy of Mayan Languages is an organization that preserves Guatemala's native dialects. It has developed a writing system for many Mayan languages that were traditionally oral, thus making it possible for Indian children to learn using textbooks, learning tools, and other publications. Since the signing of the Peace Accords, educational opportunities have expanded. More Indians are enrolling in San Carlos—Guatemala's only public university—or into any of the country's nine private universities.

Ladinos have an advantage in the Guatemalan educational system, as the medium of instruction in the majority of schools is Spanish.

79

RELIGION

THE FRANCISCAN AND DOMINICAN friars who came with the Spanish armies were not armed, but in their own way they were soldiers, intent on overpowering the Mayan paganism that they saw as the enemy. Numerous Mayan temples and holy books were destroyed. The practice of traditional beliefs was systematically outlawed and suppressed. Indians were forced into Catholicism, and those who resisted were severely punished. Despite this assault, traditional beliefs were not eradicated. While observing Catholic rituals, the indigenous people at the same time practiced their own forms of pagan worship. The Christian cross, for instance, was readily accepted in the Mayan religion. It was a symbol of the four directions—north, south, east, and west.

Even though most Guatemalans are Catholics, church ceremonies today are often conducted in a way that fits in with traditional Mayan religious expressions. This synthesis has been called Folk Catholicism. It encompasses the elements of ancestor worship that are central to Mayan religion but alien to Catholicism.

Above: **The intricately decorated San Andres Xecul Church in Quezaltenango. Traditional religious architecture and local art combine to give this church a striking facade.**

Opposite: **A simple Christian cross overlooks the city of Antigua.**

ROMAN CATHOLICISM

Roman Catholicism has had a mixed history in Guatemala. Once an integral part of the Spanish colonization of the country, its influence was severely weakened in the second half of the 19th century. The number of anticlerical measures passed by the various liberal governments curtailed the power of the church as an institution. In the 1950s and 1960s, however, the church's fortunes improved because the government

Icons of the traditional Catholic faith are still revered and are always present during religious festivals.

valued Catholicism's anticommunist stance. Yet the number of priests had declined to 500 by the 1970s, a far smaller ratio in proportion to the population than in many other Latin American countries.

Around this time, a number of priests were influenced by liberation theology, a religious movement that started in the late 20th century among Latin American clergy that emphasizes salvation as liberation from injustice. Practitioners began to speak up on behalf of the Indians and on issues of social equality. The military establishment was violently opposed to the movement. Because of that, some clerics were ordered to leave the country and in the early 1980s, about a dozen priests were murdered by right-wing military groups. Today Roman Catholicism is losing ground to evangelical Protestantism.

EVANGELICAL CHURCHES

As part of the liberal movement against Catholicism, Guatemala's president invited Protestant missionaries to the country in the late 19th century. Protestantism began to make inroads within the urban Ladino population around the 1950s. By 1983 the religions claimed to have reached over 20 percent of the population.

General Efraín Ríos Montt—a fundamentalist Christian who was president for only one year in the 1980s—directly influenced the growth of evangelism. Under his rule, rural villages were encouraged to form defense militias. Those that did not participate became key targets for government attacks. Thousands of Guatemalan peasants took refuge in evangelical churches, for it had become clear that joining one would protect them from military persecution. Today it is estimated that half the country's population has converted to evangelical worship. Only about one-third of Guatemalans are mainstream Roman Catholics.

ANCIENT BELIEFS

After reciting their prayers, these indigenous spiritual leaders prepare for a ceremonial rite at the shore of a lake.

Despite suffering centuries of religious persecution at the hands of Spanish Christians, traditional Mayan beliefs survived. Besides incorporating tribal religious observances into the Catholic religion, many of today's Guatemalan Indians still adhere to pre-Columbian notions of witchcraft and magic. Important phases in a person's life, including birth and death, are marked by ancient non-Christian ceremonies. Indian farmers in more traditional communities still use the 260-day Mayan calendar to help them determine when to plant corn. They also chant prayers and leave devotional offerings in the hope of ensuring a good yield in the coming season.

The main difference between Christianity and the Mayan religion lies in the Indian's embrace of animist beliefs—deeply ingrained thinking that many Guatemalans still cling to. While Christians believe only humans have a living soul, animism acknowledges that animals, plants, natural phenomena, and even inanimate objects contain an essence of life, too. That explains why the Indians still pray at various holy places in the mountains that are dedicated to local spirits.

This magnificent temple is known as the Temple of the Masks. It was historically the principal Mayan site, and would have staged many religious rituals.

The name of the god Itzamná is translated as "iguana house," and that could explain why he is often represented having reptilian characteristics.

MAYAN RELIGION

It is believed that the Maya thought in terms of long cycles of creation and destruction, with dominant ideas of a heaven and an underworld. Little is known about their gods, however, except that there were quite a number of them. Various gods were worshipped by people from diverse professions. For example, there was a god for beekeepers, another for hunters, and even one for comedians. It is unclear whether the Maya held one god to be a supreme creator of all life. Some evidence has credited Hunab Ku, or Itzamná, with this principal role, but others argue that both these deities are two versions of the same god who was deemed omnipotent only as a result of the imposition of Christianity on Mayan culture. Whatever the case, Itzamná does seem to occupy a special place in the hearts of the Maya. Typically portrayed as an aged, toothless figure, he has a prominent hooked nose and reptilian features.

Maya beliefs considered the earth, heaven, and underworld to be parts of one unified system. There were thirteen levels to heaven and nine to the underworld, which was called *xibalba* (shee-bahl-BAH). Each of them served a distinct role in accordance with astrological laws. Caves were treated as sacred places. Thought to be the entrances to *xibalba*, they were often richly decorated with glyphs and murals.

There was a Mayan clergy, and priests conducted ritual sacrifices of humans at specific times according to the complex Mayan calendar. Slaves and prisoners were common sacrificial victims, along with illegitimate children and orphans. Animals were also sacrificed to the gods.

The concept and understanding of time in Mayan culture was influenced by religious implications. In the Mayan calendar each measure of time—a

SHAMANS

Indians believe in supernatural powers. They also believe that holy people, called shamans, are capable of interceding with these powers. More popularly known as witch doctors, shamans acted as medicine men, magicians, and priests. An Indian who is stricken with an illness is just as likely to consult a shaman as a physician. There is a wealth of folk knowledge regarding different ways of treating illnesses, and many involve placating the spirit responsible for the  misfortune. At the birth of a child, the presence of a shaman is often considered as essential as the attendance of a midwife. A shaman also officiates at marriage ceremonies and funerals. At a cemetery, the shaman rotates the coffin in different directions to fool any evil spirit that might be awaiting the newly dead. A traditional Indian farmer also consults a shaman before embarking on a new planting cycle.

Most, though not all, shamans are men, and they have their own costumes. They usually carry a small bag containing bits of mirror and pottery, red beans or corn kernels, and other implements used in making prophecies or casting fortunes. Some shamans still consult the ancient Mayan calendar when calculating propitious days or performing religious rites.

day, for example—was envisaged as temporarily belonging to a divine figure who "carried" that period of time until it was passed onto another god. This applied not only to days but also to years, centuries, and even longer eras. This created never-ending cycles wherein gods could influence life through their command over specific periods of time.

POPOL VUH

The *Popol Vuh* (poh-POL VOO) is an impressive account of Mayan religious thought. It was translated from Mayan into Latin in the 16th century by Indian priests who had been taught Spanish and Latin by Dominican friars. For almost 150 years it lay unknown. Eventually a Spanish missionary discovered the text. Instead of destroying it, he chose to copy the account and wrote a Spanish translation. His version is the one that has survived and, though incomplete, it remains a vital source of information about Mayan religion.

This figure was used as an incense burner during religious celebrations by the Maya. It was discovered in one of the temples at Tikal.

The *Popol Vuh* has been translated into over 40 languages. It ends with the arrival of the Spanish, having begun with the story of how the gods had tried, but failed, to create humans, first out of earth and then of wood. The wooden beings did not melt in water such as those made from earth, but their inability to think or to thank the gods resulted in their destruction. Eventually, the gods succeeded in creating human beings by using corn to make flesh, then mixing it with water to make blood.

A religious parade led by a local *cofradías*. The banner is carried to identify the brotherhood, followed by a religious float.

In a metaphorical sense, traditional Indians still see themselves as *Men of Maize*, the title of a famous 1949 novel by Guatemalan writer Miguel Ángel Asturias, which was awarded the 1967 Nobel Prize for Literature. Posters appeared after the 1976 earthquake depicting a single ear of corn and the slogan *"Hombre de maíz, levantate!"* (Man of corn, arise!)

COFRADÍAS

Cofradías (coh-frah-DEE-ass) are religious brotherhoods of lay members. First established by the Spanish, these associations of Indians had a primary responsibility—ensuring the welfare of the image that represented their community's saint. On the day of a religious festival, it was the duty of the *cofradías* to carry the saint's image, often a thinly disguised pagan god renamed as a Christian saint. Toward the end of the 19th century, the Catholic church's influence waned following the expulsion of the archbishop of Guatemala. People continued worshiping, nonetheless, and the clergy's function was filled by *cofradías* even though they had been outlawed in an 1872 presidential decree. No longer considered illegal, these brotherhoods are still devoted to caring for their particular community's saint. During religious festivals members of the *cofradías*

Parishoners in Antigua carrying incense burners while walking in a procession commemorating Semana Santa.

take their place at the head of the procession, which is a matter of great local status.

The chief *cofrade* holds a very prestigious position in the village community, and like all members of the brotherhood, he is elected on an annual basis. He attains his position after many years of service and only after gaining the local community's respect and trust.

New members usually join as teenagers, carrying out civic duties such as keeping the village square clean. They gradually progress through different stages of responsibility and positions within the brotherhood, according to their age. Women sometimes operate their own *cofradías*, but generally, they move up through the ranks alongside their spouses.

SEMANA SANTA

Semana Santa (seh-MA-na SAN-ta) is Spanish for Holy Week, which is the week before Easter. It is the occasion for some of Guatemala's most important religious celebrations. A procession takes place on Palm Sunday, the Sunday before Easter that marks Christ's entry into Jerusalem. This is the start of a weeklong devotion that culminates on Good Friday with

SAINT MAXIMÓN

The fusion of Roman Catholicism and Maya paganism is clearly illustrated through the worship of Saint Maximón in Santiago Atitlán. Dressed in Western clothes, the saint's image is the focus of an annual procession during Holy Week, the only time his effigy is paraded in public. Worshipers pour alcohol over the image, and it is customary to blow cigar smoke around him. Don't let such lighthearted gestures obscure the fact that these people are staunchly devoted to their Saint Maximón.

The saint is also called San Simón. Some have tried to identify him with Judas Iscariot and Pedro de Alvarado, the Spanish conquistador who conquered Guatemala. He is also associated with the ancient Mayan god Mam. After Holy Week, it is the duty of a *cofradía* member—a different one is chosen each year—to house the saint in his home. Visitors who wish to see Saint Maximón are expected to bring some rum and cigars or cigarettes as a gift.

a major procession marking the occasion of Christ's crucifixion. Easter Sunday, which takes place two days later, celebrates the belief that Christ rose from the dead. Like Christmas, Easter is a time for joyful gatherings of families and friends.

The statues of saints that are carried during Semana Santa processions are reverently dressed in Indian costumes, another interesting example of how orthodox Christianity has merged with more traditional Mayan practices.

Antigua, the original capital, hosted the earliest Semana Santa celebrations in the late 17th century. These annual festivities were first introduced by the Spanish conqueror Pedro de Alvarado. When the capital was relocated to Guatemala City, following the 1773 earthquake that destroyed much of Antigua, it was decided that all unbroken religious art should be moved there as well. This caused a great deal of consternation among the local *cofradías*, and they hid a number of statues. Some of the statues being carried in Antigua's Semana Santa processions today date back to the 17th century and are said to be the very ones that were spirited away by their caretakers after the earthquake.

POLLO AL CARBON
*Consomé
*¼ de pollo
*Ensalada
*Papas fritas
*Chirmol

Q24.95

CHURRASCO
*Consomé
*Viuda sin hueso
*Papa a la parrilla
*Maiz dulce
*Chirmol

Q24.95

LANGUAGE

SPANISH, THE OFFICIAL LANGUAGE of Guatemala, is spoken by only about 60 percent of the population, while different Indian dialects, numbering over 20, account for the remaining 40 percent. When the Spanish arrived in the 16th century, the predominant Mayan language was called Cholan, which was related to the Yucatec language of the Yucatán Peninsula. Cholan is the ancestral language of the Indian dialects that are widely used in Guatemala today.

The Indian dialect spoken by a Guatemalan is an important indicator of the speaker's ethnic identity. In the past, Indians were identified by a combination of dress and language, but nowadays the use of their distinct mother tongue alone indicates that they still see themselves as Indians.

Above: **Village men reading a Bible. Due to the religious zeal of Guatemalans, many in the rural countryside enjoy reading the Scriptures.**

Opposite: **A signboard menu written in Spanish. The knowledge of Spanish is important in Guatemala as it is the official language of the country affecting schools and businesses.**

Spanish is spoken by all Ladinos, while a growing number of Indians speak both Spanish and an Indian language. In the highlands it is usual for Ladino residents to have some ability with the local Indian dialect, but it is rare for them to be able to speak the two languages fluently. Generally, more Indians than Ladinos are bilingual. That is partly because the main medium of instruction in schools is Spanish, which means Indians learn it as their second language. Ladinos usually learn English as a second language, since they are not taught Indian languages in schools at all. Another way in which Indians, especially males, become bilingual is through their exposure to different languages at work. Outside of Indian villages, the ability to converse in Spanish is essential to find work in towns and cities. Finally, compulsory military service for males means that the Indian men called up for military service find themselves having to understand and use Spanish.

SPANISH

The Spanish language was taken to Guatemala by the Spanish conquistadors in the 16th century. The Spanish clergy then taught the language to the Indians to facilitate their mission of converting the local population to Christianity and to supervise their forced labor. A similar process took place across most of Central and South America. Although the basic vocabulary and grammar of Latin American Spanish is identical to that of modern Spanish, there are some differences in pronunciation. The most obvious disparity is the absence of the soft *s* found in European Spanish.

Both Latin American and European Spanish are relatively easy languages to pronounce, with the stress generally falling on the penultimate, or second to last syllable. Words that end with the letters *r*, *d*, *l*, and *z* stress the last syllable unless there is an accent in the word.

Guatemala has a number of Spanish-language newspapers. Popular dailies include Siglo Veintiuno, Prensa Libre, *and* El Periódico. El Regional *is a weekly paper that is published in both Spanish and Maya.*

Spanish is the medium of instruction in schools, which explains why about 60 percent of Guatemalans are fluent in the Spanish language.

The word "gringo" is derived from *griego* (gree-AY-go), the Spanish word for Greek. It has come to mean any nonlocal person in general, and a North American or European in particular. There was a time when the word was used, especially in Mexico, in an abusive and insulting way, but nowadays the term is used in a neutral manner to simply indicate a tourist or visitor.

ANCIENT MAYA

The ancient Mayan writing system has survived mostly in the form of stone inscriptions. Sadly, only four Mayan books have weathered the ravages of time. It is clear that the Maya placed great importance on writing—the god who may have been their supreme spiritual force, Itzamná, was also regarded as the inventor of writing.

Most Mayan writing has now been deciphered, yet uncertainty still remains over the linguistic nature of many of the 1,500 glyphs that make up the written language. Mayan glyphs consist of a central symbol with various additions placed around it, or even within the central symbol. It is generally agreed that most glyphs contained a phonetic value, as the symbols probably affected how they were pronounced, but reconstructing how the language actually sounded remains a scholarly mystery. At the same time, each glyph also contains an ideographic element—an ideogram being a character that represents an idea—and this feature has been more successfully interpreted by historians and linguists. This means that even though we do not know how the language was spoken, we can still read and translate the writing based on the meanings embedded in the ideograms.

Stone glyphs such as these provide a lasting record of the ancient Mayan language.

ANCIENT WRITING

Apart from inscriptions on stone, the only original examples of the Mayan language are found in four ancient manuscripts. The text appears on long strips of paper called codices. They were made from the pulverized bark of fig trees, or deer skin, cotton cloth, and maguey paper. These strips measured less than 10 inches (25 cm) across but they stretched over several yards in length. The length allowed each strip of paper to be folded back-to-back, concertina-like, and images of books on pottery show that the folded pages were covered with jaguar skin, revealing the high valuation placed by Mayans on their literature.

The Maya wrote with brushes and pens that were made from turkey feathers. Their writing was often exuberantly colored with paints made from vegetables and minerals.

MODERN MAYA

The distribution of the Indian dialects spoken in Guatemala varies geographically. The western half of the country has the greatest linguistic diversity. The Quichéan who live in the midwestern highlands are the largest group of Indian speakers.

The Academy of Mayan Languages was founded in 1986. It preserves and encourages Mayan literacy by conducting literacy programs for Indians across Guatemala. The academy has helped to develop a uniform Mayan alphabet for the various Indian languages. Its council consists of representatives from each of the 23 Mayan language groups, and one of its ongoing tasks is the compilation of dictionaries for every language.

ARAWAKAN LANGUAGES

Arawakan is a language family of 65 South American dialects, many of which are still spoken today. A small number of Guatemalans, mainly the Garifuna, are conversant in Arawakan. These dialects once were widespread and were spoken as far north as Florida and as far south as the present border between Argentina and Paraguay, as well as in the Caribbean islands. It was the first Indian language heard by the Spanish when they landed in the Americas. The words canoe, tobacco, and maize (corn) all came from Arawakan.

BODY LANGUAGE

Body language is generally more overt, or noticeable, in urban areas than in the countryside. Direct gesturing with the hand, however, is discouraged in all situations, partly because hand gestures are considered rude and offensive. This reticence is not unique to Guatemalan society. It is a fairly common social norm across Latin America. If there is a need to point toward someone, it is more likely to be accomplished by pursing one's lips in the direction of the person to be indicated. To call someone over, the hand is held out then waved downward and toward the body. This modest action is considered rather blatant, although tolerated. To attract someone's attention in a more discreet manner, a tssst sound is made in the direction of the person being signaled.

When it comes to courting, young couples are generally quite conservative. Open displays of affection such as hugging or kissing are very uncommon. This is especially true in rural areas where holding hands is considered the most brazen indication of a relationship.

Among friends, hand gestures to emphasize a point or to attract attention are seen as rude and are seldom used.

95

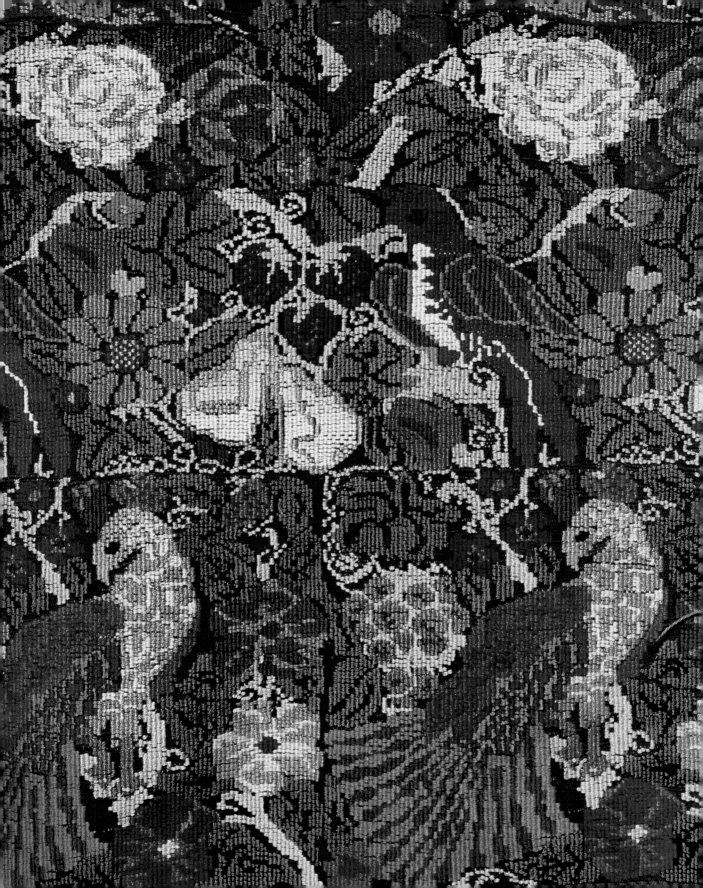

ARTS

GUATEMALAN CULTURE FINDS EXPRESSION in a variety of art forms. The artistry of the ancient Maya is evident in the architecture of their temples and palaces that have survived the passing centuries. These monuments remain the most visible examples of Mayan creativity. The ruins of Uaxactun in Petén reflect late pre-Classic influences, whereas the Classic site of Tikal shines as the crown jewel of Mayan architecture.

Contemporary Guatemalan culture flourishes in the areas of literature and folk art such as weaving and dressmaking. Weaving has a long Mayan history dating back to pre-Columbian times when vegetable fibers were used as thread and insects and minerals were used to make dyes. No samples have survived, but numerous depictions on the frescos and relief sculptures of Mayan buildings show that ancient Mayan dress was similar to the kind of attire that is in use today.

Left: **Hand carved masks for sale in a typical Guatemalan market featuring locally crafted articles.**

Opposite: **An intricately woven cloth pattern from Guatemala.**

Stelae like this one were used by the Mayans to record significant events. They can be found around temples, usually near a plaza or open courtyard. Historians have treasured these ancient public records.

ART IN STONE

Mayan art is at its grandest and most compelling when expressed through stone architecture. Huge pyramid temples were constructed long centuries ago using limestone blocks over a core mound of rubble. They were built without the help of wheels or metal tools or other technology, yet all were aligned in such a way that they allowed for sophisticated and accurate astronomical readings. Large, single-story palaces containing many rooms were built, but judging by their cramped quarters it appears that the elite lived elsewhere, using the palaces only for special occasions.

In Classic times, the temples and palaces were always built around a large plaza, upon which rows of stone slabs, or stelae, were placed. These carved stone pillars were richly illustrated, usually with a male figure in some form of ceremonial dress, and preserved the record of an important date, such as that of a royal accession or a powerful official's birthday.

The ruins of Tikal—one of the largest Mayan cities and ceremonial centers—are located in the rain forest of Petén. Tikal was first occupied around 600 B.C., but its grandeur dates to the Classic period (A.D. 300–900). By the 10th century, Tikal had been mysteriously abandoned by all who lived and toiled there. The great pyramids, palaces, and plazas dotting the site were built between A.D. 600 and 800. The most important buildings are ceremonial in nature. They occupy an area of about 1 square mile (2.6 square km), but excavations have revealed a surrounding area of about 6 square miles (15.5 square km) that contained smaller residential buildings surrounding the temples.

TIKAL

The center of ancient Tikal is a great plaza occupying an area of about 2 acres (0.8 ha). Rows of stelae stand like sentinels to the north of the plaza. The Temple of the Great Jaguar, christened Temple I by archaeologists, sits at the east end. It once contained the tomb of an eighth-century Tikal ruler whose name translates as Lord Chocolate. To the west is Temple II, which may contain the as-yet-undiscovered tomb of Lord Chocolate's wife. North of the plaza is a structure known as the North Acropolis, which contains temples and a maze of interconnecting stairways and passages. Excavations have revealed two giant masks and a burial chamber in which a ruler was buried along with nine servants, a crocodile, and turtles.

A ball court is located south of the plaza, along with a large, 4-acre (1.6-ha) site known as the Central Acropolis, which contains a number of palaces. To the west of the Central Acropolis are two more temples, including Temple IV, one of the tallest buildings ever constructed by a Native American culture.

The great temples and pyramids are astonishing when one considers that they were built without using wheels or draft animals to transport the massive stone blocks, some of which weighed as much as 60 tons (61,000 kg). Questions of how these mighty blocks were quarried and placed in position may never be answered. Still, some artists have tried to provide impressions of what it might have looked in thé past.

Relief carvings adorned temple walls and ceremonial items such as thrones. They give a striking impression of the facial features of the people and the clothes and jewelry they wore.

MAYAN ART FORMS

Besides the construction of large temples and palaces, evidence of Mayan skills are found on a smaller scale in low-relief carvings—a technique in which the design stands out from the surface. Mayan artists perfected this art form on their stelae and on temple panels.

Pottery was painted in fine detail and in many colors. It was common to fire the clay at relatively low temperatures in order to achieve the desired colors. This reduced the useful life of the vessel, but the artistic effect was considered more important. Mayan pottery that originated around A.D. 700 is regarded as some of the finest creations of ancient times. Surprisingly, the potter's wheel was not known to the Mayan world.

Mayan artists thought of jade as their most precious material. Fine, low-relief carving was carefully inscribed onto jade surfaces using tiny chisels and cane drills. Many examples of jade jewelry have been unearthed from Mayan tombs. The highly prized stone was also inlaid in shells and stone. Jade was even inlaid into a person's teeth as a mark of social superiority.

MAYAN LITERATURE

The four original Mayan texts that have survived the ravages of time are all concerned with religious matters, as well as calendrical and astronomical calculations such as lunar eclipses and the cycles of Venus. Spanish sources have described Mayan writings on history, myth, and science. Regrettably, it seems that a rich literature has been lost forever, owing partly to the zeal with which Spanish priests destroyed Mayan books that were perceived to be pagan heresy. Stone inscriptions mostly consist of records of various rulers and their families—their noble names deserving the permanence of stone. These also reflect the common Mayan concern with calculating exact dates.

A secondary source of Mayan literature exists because Spanish missionaries taught their language to some Indians who used it to translate their own writings into Spanish. This is how the famous *Popol Vuh* managed to survive.

TEXTILE ARTS

Although it has humble origins, the woven cloth produced in the highlands can be considered an art form in itself. Despite the increasing availability and popularity of machine-manufactured garments, many village women still make their own outfits, using a backstrap loom. One end of the loom is tied to a stationary object and the other is fastened behind the weaver's back to give tension. The loom consists of wooden boards around which the lengthwise threads, or warp, are wound. A stick allows every other warp thread to be lifted so that the crosswise thread, called the weft, can be passed through the space and tamped down. The technology is simple, yet it allows intricate and brightly colored patterns to be woven

A fascinating aspect of Mayan temples is the way in which the buildings, or parts of the building complex, were aligned so as to facilitate celestial observations. For example, a particular temple door or window would have been placed to provide a view of a star or planet in an especially auspicious position on a certain day.

A woman weaving on a backstrap loom, used by Guatemalan women all over the region to produce brightly colored and finely woven fabrics.

into the material. Later, other patterns may be embroidered onto the cloth, adding yet more color and complexity to the final product. The traditional blouses, called *huipils*, are made by sewing together two or more pieces of handwoven cloth.

The backstrap loom is traditionally used only by women, while men use foot-treadled looms. The foot loom, which was introduced by the Spanish, permits the weaving of larger pieces of cloth. Foot pedals, connected to the rods that control the warp, are used to lift the threads alternately to form a space. The weft yarns are fed through the space by way of hand-held wooden shuttles.

MUSIC

Music has always been a central feature in Mayan culture, and there are many references to singing and flute playing in the *Popol Vuh*. The most common traditional instrument in Guatemala is the marimba, a percussion instrument that is similar to a vibraphone. First introduced

to the Caribbean peoples from Africa via the slave trade, it is now very popular across Latin America.

The marimba was originally played by striking gourds of varying sizes with drumsticks to produce different notes. The modern instrument comes with its own double keyboard and wooden tubes that can produce different resonances. At festival time, a traveling marimba orchestra, complete with brass accompaniments, usually arrives on the back of an open truck in any village that cannot muster its own team of musicians. Towns are more likely to have their own resident orchestras.

Indians play other instruments at ceremonial occasions. During religious processions the *chirimía* (cher-er-MIA), a flutelike instrument, is often deployed. It produces a sad tone somewhat similar to the oboe. Various types of drums are played, and many are simply made by stretching the skin of an animal over a suitably shaped frame of wood. Rhythm is also produced by shaking gourds filled with beans or seeds.

The marimba produces a melodic sound and played together with other instruments, is an important part of any Guatemalan celebration. A traveling band such as this plays to appreciative audiences all over the country.

An ornately dressed dancer lights the fireworks in preparation for the Dance of the Conquest.

DANCE

Dance is an essential component in most festivals and is often fairly unstructured. The dances are usually performed by men only, who dress up for the occasion in elaborate padded costumes, hideous masks, elaborate wigs, and plumed hats. Such costumes have to be rented, and the choice of dance often depends on how much money the village can afford to spend on a set of costumes. Some dances may last for hours. They have sometimes been compared to endurance marathons because exhausted dancers are often barely able to stay on their feet toward the end.

More structured dances, requiring greater practice, take place in traditional Indian towns, including Todos Santos and Chichicastenango. A common dance, Baile de la Conquista (BY-leh day la con-QUIS-ta), or the Dance of the Conquest, reenacts the encounter between the Spanish and the Maya. Dancers representing the Spanish wear masks painted to represent the pale skin of the Europeans, with large white noses attached. The dance, first choreographed by a Spanish priest in 1542, climaxes with the victory of the Spanish, but nowadays Indians enjoy the spectacle with little regard for its historical references.

Another representation of Spanish dominance, the Dance of the Volcanoes, also celebrates a Spanish military victory over rebellious Indians that took place near the volcano Agua in 1526. The Quiché Indians have their own dance, known as the Dance of the Black Ones, dedicated primarily to a figure known as Black Elk, or the Black One. Black Elk is considered to be one of the greatest religious thinkers ever produced by native North American Indians. His account perhaps remains the most useful portrayal of the age-old Lakota religion, as represented through its recounting of Black Elk's great vision.

WRITERS

In recent decades, Guatemala has produced two notable authors. Miguel Ángel Asturias won the Nobel Prize for Literature in 1967 and Rigoberta Menchú was awarded the Nobel Peace Prize in 1992. Both writers have discussed their country's plight and politics. Menchú's book, *I, Rigoberta Menchú*, tells the true and heartrending story of how the Indians suffered at the hands of the military authorities. The novels of Asturias, who was born in 1899,

Nobel Prize winner for literature Miguel Ángel Asturias.

contain a mystical overtone. Together they raise a powerful social protest on behalf of the Maya. He has been called the inventor of magical realism, a term used to describe a genre of South American literature that fuses a present reality with the supernatural. As a young writer, Asturias lived in Paris and was greatly influenced by surrealism. He also translated the *Popol Vuh* while in the French capital. His first internationally renowned book, translated into English as *Legends of Guatemala*, chronicled the cultural life of the Maya before the Spanish arrived. After his return to Guatemala, he wrote his major novels, beginning with *El señor presidente* in 1946. An English translation, titled *The President*, was published in 1964. Then followed his other novel, *Hombres de maiz*, in 1949. The translated version in 1949 was titled *Men of Maize*. Considered his most important novel, *Men of Maize* narrates the terrible plight of the Indian peasants. Asturias went on to write an epic trilogy about the exploitation that the Indians suffered while working in the United Fruit Company's banana plantations. He died in 1974.

Rigoberta Menchú was born in 1959. At the age of 8, she had to work on a coffee plantation and witnessed her brother dying of malnutrition. When she was 20, another brother was murdered by the army. Her father died when the army set fire to the Spanish Embassy building that he, along with a group of political activists, had been occupying. Following this, her mother was kidnapped and murdered by the army. She became a refugee in Mexico, where she wrote the harrowing story of her life in the book *I, Rigoberta Menchú*. The Nobel Committee, in awarding her the prize for literature, described her work as "a vivid symbol of peace and reconciliation across ethnic, cultural, and social dividing lines." The country's military rulers were upset by her momentous award. Further controversy arose when David Stoll's autobiography questioned the authenticity of her account. Many academics, nevertheless, have supported Menchú's testimony and her work on behalf of indigenous people. Today the humanitarian ambassador occupies a special place in the hearts of most Guatemalan Maya and the political left.

Another notable contemporary writer, Mario Roberto Morales, also chronicles his country's social and political conditions. Critically admired for his experimental writing style, Morales's most recent work consists of 24 parts that combine nonfiction with fiction. Excerpts from pre-Columbian religious texts and testimonies by contemporary Indians have been integrated with the story of an Indian boy who was forced to join the army after his father was murdered by the military.

Guatemala's 1992 Nobel Peace Prize laureate and social activist, Rigoberta Menchú, remains widely honored among the Maya.

COLONIAL ART

Guatemala's colonial art is best represented by the old churches and assorted buildings that the Spanish built in the 16th and 17th centuries. The town of Antigua—original capital of the Spanish—preserves many splendid examples, including the ruins of the Cathedral of San José, started in 1680. Originally it housed an impressive 18 chapels, 5 naves, and a huge dome, but a number of earthquakes caused the walls to collapse. Only 2 of the chapels have been restored.

Another church, Iglecia La Merced, has survived relatively unscathed after a series of earthquakes. Its intricately ornamented facade—one of the best examples of colonial architecture—continues to amaze visitors worldwide. After Antigua's being declared a World Heritage Site, steps are being taken to conserve more of its rich architecture. Although the complete restoration of many buildings is unlikely, preservation of the more important ruins means that colonial architectural styles will remain intact over many generations to come.

The architecture of many buildings, such as this church in Antigua, stand as a legacy to Spanish colonial design.

LEISURE

THE TYPICAL GUATEMALAN toils hard throughout the week. Taking time off to play is considered a luxury. Only a tiny fraction of the population can afford a week's vacation or a holiday abroad.

Sunday is an important day of rest. Except for street markets, virtually all businesses are closed. In the morning, many people attend a church service dressed in their best, and the afternoon is spent relaxing with the family.

There is a clear split between the leisure activities that wealthy urbanites residing in the capital indulge in and those of the rural population. Guatemala City has an entertainment area known as Zone 10 where clubs and discos are located. In rural areas, people are more likely to relax by visiting among friends. Women may spend their leisure moments creating handicrafts.

Above: **A soldier playing foosball with the local children. While the people in Guatemala City take advantage of the many opportunities for sport and leisure, there are not many facilities in the rural parts of the country. That is why the local festivals and celebrations provide most of the entertainment for the rural population.**

Opposite: **A young woman practicing yoga poses in the Guatemalan wilderness.**

SOCIALIZING

Socializing at leisure is an important activity for both Indians and Ladinos. People find time during the course of a day to talk and relax with friends and acquaintances. Only a small group of wealthy elites organize dinner parties or cocktail gatherings. Market days are especially important occasions for people to meet on a regular basis, and this holds true for merchants and shoppers alike. It's common to have two vendors manning their stalls side by side in a village square and selling identical goods, but they are often more interested in socializing with each other than in competing for sales.

Village festivals also reinforce community bonds by bringing together family members who may otherwise be working in different parts of

Men playing an ancient Mayan ball game at the Iximche ruins of an original court.

the country. Religious occasions and festive celebrations fulfill a larger social purpose by providing the rare opportunity for people to escape the monotonous grind of daily work. The nights just before a festival are often convivial occasions when people socialize with drinks or dance to a live marimba orchestra.

In urban areas, young people, especially Ladinos, socialize in a way that is similar to their North American contemporaries. By the age of 14, many young people have found their own social circles. They often get together with their friends outside of school. Leisure time is spent eating together or visiting the local movie theater. Watching the latest Hollywood blockbuster is one of the most popular entertainment options for teenagers in the capital.

BALL GAMES

Guatemalans' passion for ball games such as soccer and basketball may well have ancestral origins. The most popular game among the ancient Maya seems to have been *pok-a-tok*, a team game for which special ball courts were built. The game involved trying to place a rubber or stone ball through a ring placed just above the players' heads on the wall of the court. The rules banned touching the ball with either hands or feet, and it had to be bounced off from any other parts of the body. Players wore protective padding. While the stakes were often very high in terms of cash and property, there was also an element of fun because

it was traditional for the winning team to claim the clothing of any of the spectators who were slow enough to be caught when the game was over. More alarming, there is reason to believe that losing players were sometimes sacrificed.

SOCCER

Sports are an important leisure activity for young Guatemalans. Soccer, or *fútbol*, ranks as the most popular sport, and the media always covers important matches. There is a professional soccer league. Each season spectators and fans avidly follow the fortunes of different teams in their struggles to become the league champions. The entire country celebrated when its national soccer team advanced to the second round of the 2002 World Cup preliminaries.

Soccer matches, especially important ones held at the capital's Olympic Stadium, are noisy but cheerful events. Setting off firecrackers is a traditional way of expressing jubilation following a victory. Most spectators stand while watching a game. Refreshments are sold during matches by vendors who carry large coolers full of beer, which is dispensed into small plastic bags and drunk with a straw.

A group of boys enjoying a friendly soccer game. Soccer (*fútbol*) is enjoyed in many forms. The national league is followed closely by most Guatemalans, and many young boys dream of playing professionally.

Guatemala's most famous footballer, Carlos Ruíz Gutierrez, is a familiar face in major league Soccer. He was the Most Valuable Player (2002) and a Golden Boot winner (2002 and 2003).

111

Two men enjoying the scenic view of Lake Atitlán and its surrounding volcanic mountains.

Schools do not train students in soccer, the way football is coached in American schools, but soccer is always featured as an option in physical education programs for boys. It is rare for a girl or woman to play soccer. At school, girls usually play basketball and volleyball.

LAKESIDE LEISURE

A favorite weekend getaway for urban residents, the picturesque Lake Amatitlán is about 10 miles (16 km) south of Guatemala City. Buses depart from the capital regularly—as many as five an hour—and are usually crowded with families traveling to picnic at the lakefront. In their enjoyment, they remain unperturbed by the ominous presence of Pacaya, an active volcano on the southern slopes of the lake. In fact, Pacaya's beauty at night is a major attraction. People like to watch the vibrant colors around the mountain cone as it bubbles away, casting an orange glow in the dark night sky. During the day boat trips across the lake are very popular, but sadly, much of the lake has been polluted.

The ancient Maya celebrated the summer solstice—the time in June when the sun is farthest north of the equator—by going to Amatitlán to bathe. They also prayed at an altar in a nearby forest. Rituals intended to placate the gods and ensure a good harvest included sacrificing children in the lake. Nowadays, with the coming of May the area around the lakeside becomes a site for various leisure activities, ranging from dancing and live music to water sports—defying the pollution. Special decorated boxes, filled with sweets, are sold by park vendors during the warm months.

Lake Amatitlán's famous cousin, Lake Atitlán, occasionally hosts sailing tournaments. Lately, Atitlán has been gaining prominence as a high-altitude scuba diving destination.

DANCING AND MUSIC

Sophisticated young Guatemalans love to dance. In the capital's nightclubs, the most popular forms of dancing are salsa and disco. Salsa is a type of music as well as a dance, combining Latin jazz with rock music to produce a fast and energetic rhythm ideally suited for the disco floor. Discos are not usually found outside the capital city. In smaller towns and rural areas, music and dance are often confined to festival days and nights only. Religious holidays are the occasions for displays of folk dances in traditional costumes, the most common dance being the *Baile de la Conquista* (BY-leh day la con-QUIS-ta), the Dance of the Conquest, which dramatizes the defeat of the Indians and pokes fun at the Spanish.

Elaborate costumes make the Dance of the Conquest a spectacle not to be missed. Dressed as Spanish conquistadores, the dancers reenact the arrival of the Spanish in Guatemala.

FESTIVALS

COUNTLESS FESTIVALS ARE CELEBRATED in Guatemala, and while most of them have a religious foundation, they also provide occasions for social relaxation and merriment. Lent is traditionally a period of abstinence and restraint, but the week before Lent is often carnival time in Ladino communities. The week before Easter is the most important occasion, even more significant than Christmas. It is a time when most Guatemalans return to their own villages to prepare to observe Easter with their families. Some aspects of the religious festivals cast light on the unique way in which traditional Mayan beliefs have merged with Catholicism.

FIESTAS

The Spanish word fiesta (fee-EST-a), meaning a party or festival, was absorbed into the English language with the same cheery meaning. Just about every village and town in Guatemala devotes at least one day in each year to its particular saint, although celebrations frequently extend over a period of several weeks. In urban Ladino areas, fiestas are characterized by religious processions, which are accompanied by musicians playing in the streets. Sometimes a local beauty contest is featured.

In areas where indigenous Indians make up a majority, the fiesta merges with customary pre-Columbian forms of celebration. Traditionally dressed participants participate in dancing and merrymaking. In the town of Rabinal, for example, dance dramas reenacting ancient Mayan rituals are performed. Wherever a fiesta takes place, dramatic bursts of fireworks light up the night sky, adding to a party atmosphere. During festival times, more food and drink is consumed than at any other time of the year.

Above: **A masked dancer participates in the Dance of the Bulls held on the first day of Guatemala's annual patron saint celebration, which culminates on All Saints' Day and ends on the Day of the Dead, or All Souls' Day. To add to the fun, these events also feature carousels or ferris wheels.**

Opposite: **Crowds gather to watch the stately Easter parade procession.**

CHICHICASTENANGO'S FIESTA

The town of Chichicastenango is renowned for its Indian character. The annual fiesta honoring Saint Thomas on December 21 is one of Guatemala's most spectacular festivals. As many as 10,000 participants join in the celebrations that last for three days. A succession of parades weave through the narrow streets. These are headed by local Indians wearing traditional garments, which are woven from black wool and richly embroidered with Mayan symbols.

Some traditional dances may last many hours. A special pole is erected, around which ritual dances are performed. In the dance known as *palo volador* (PAH-lo vo-la-DOR, pole flying), men tied to the ends of ropes at the top of a 65-foot (20-m) pole spin themselves through the air at dizzying—and dangerous—speeds to unwind the ropes and descend to the ground.

Festivities form an important part of a community's regular life. Energetic parades and dances provide participants with opportunities to meet one another and socialize. On the morning of Saint Thomas's Day, for instance, families gather and all babies born in the previous year are communally baptized at the village church. As dusk falls, the atmosphere bursts alive with the colors, sounds, and scents of fireworks and the smoke of festive cooking.

SEMANA SANTA

Easter's Semana Santa (seh-MA-na SAN-ta), or Holy Week, is Guatemala's most important religious festival. The week before Holy Week, known as Semana de Dolores (seh-MA-na day doll-ORE-ez, the Week of Sorrow), is a busy time of preparation. Entire villages and churches are swept clean before being decorated with bright flowers and colored streamers. The costumes that dress the holy images are cleaned and repaired, while rehearsals are scheduled for the coming processions and parades.

Holy Week is characterized by huge, colorful processions, giant floats on which devotional statues of saints are carried aloft, and the liberal use of incense. In some of the larger towns where more extravagant processions are the norm—Antigua being the most famous in this respect—the biggest floats weigh as much as 3 tons and require a team of 60 or more men to carry them.

Village communities each have their own ways of celebrating Holy Week. The village of Chiantla, in the western highlands, blends the sacred with the profane. Based on the idea of the apostles' escaping from the Good Friday procession and hiding in the countryside, the observances include a mock manhunt where all the "apostles" are eventually escorted back

During the Holy Week procession, statues of Christ are displayed to commemorate his crucifixion. Bright costumes and flowers are also placed onto the figure to express devotion and to add color.

The Thursday before Easter is the only day in the year that Indians deliberately refrain from eating corn. Deliveries of special bread are made to villages, and that bread is eaten in commemoration of Christ's meal at the Last Supper.

Residents of Guatemala City look on as a Christmas tree given by the beer company Gallo and fireworks light the sky.

to the procession. The character of Judas—the apostle who betrayed Christ to the authorities—is often represented by a scarecrow. This figure is mocked and insulted before being put on trial and burned for his act of betrayal. Sometimes the scarecrow is tied to a donkey by a rope and dragged through the streets.

The days of Holy Week tend to follow a familiar pattern year after year. Wednesday is usually market day, when villagers will buy sufficient supplies of food and flowers to mark the special occasion. The following two days are devoted to religious processions. On the evening of Good Friday, after a commemoration of the act of crucifixion, the Christ figure is returned to the church. Saturday is quieter, which allows people to relax and enjoy themselves. Jubilant church services are held on Easter Sunday.

CHRISTMAS

The celebration of the birth of Christ is a major religious festival for Christians, but in Guatemala, Christmas celebrations rate second in popularity to Semana Santa. Public events and spectacles are muted. One reason may be that Easter, marking as it does winter's end and spring's arrival, resonates with ancient Mayan fertility rites in a way that Christmas does not. It is only in Ladino towns that one part of the Christmas story, the search for lodgings by Mary and Joseph, is reenacted. Known as *las posadas* (las po-SAH-das)—Spanish for a shelter or lodging—it takes place over nine evenings leading up to December 25. Christmas in Guatemala

ANTIGUA'S *ALFOMBRAS*

The city of Antigua is famous for its splendid Semana Santa festivities, notably the *alfombras* (al-FOM-bras)—Spanish for carpet. The main procession street and the area outside churches are "carpeted" in elaborate patterns made with sawdust and flower petals. When the procession has passed by, some people collect handfuls of the *alfombras*, believing it has become endowed with miraculous properties.

Alfombras can be found all over Guatemala at festival time, but the people of Antigua seem determined to maintain their exemplary reputation in this event. More than 200 people work through the night, crafting the main religious images and patterns. Individual households also create

alfombras outside their houses if the procession is to pass by their doorstep. The Procession of the Roman Soldiers takes place in the early hours of the day before Good Friday, when participants run through the streets announcing Christ's death penalty and are followed by men on horseback representing the Roman army. When the festival is over, the results of everyone's painstaking labor are swept away to cleanse the city.

has none of the commercial ballyhoo it has acquired in North America and Europe. More concerned with making ends meet day by day, the vast majority of the population lacks resources, particularly extra money, to buy presents.

ALL SAINTS' AND ALL SOULS' DAYS

November 1 is All Saints' Day and November 2 is regarded as All Souls' Day, also known as the Day of the Dead. Although both days are religious festivals, they are celebrated and greeted across Guatemala with lively parties. Some towns are famous for their fiestas at these times.

Huge kites fill the sky on All Souls' Day. Setting them aloft requires great skill. They are believed to relieve the suffering of souls not yet admitted to heaven.

Any town with the name of Todos Santos, or All Saints, will make a special effort to commemorate All Saints' Day, and people flock to that town from the surrounding countryside to view the famous horse races that are organized there. The festival begins with a stampede of horses across a large field. On the following day, prayers and rituals are conducted in the cemetery to assuage the souls of the dead.

In the small town of Santiago Sacatepéquez, the townspeople make huge paper and bamboo kites in preparation for the Day of the Dead. On November 2 the kites are released to symbolize the liberation of dead souls suffering in purgatory. The kites can measure as wide as 20 feet (6 m) across and it takes a team effort to get them airborne.

THE ESQUIPULAS PILGRIMAGE

Located on the border with Honduras and El Salvador, the small eastern town of Esquipulas attracts thousands of devotees from Central America every January 15. The focus of prayer is a statue of Christ carved from a block of balsam and placed inside the church in 1595. One legend relates that the statue was inspired by a vision of a black Christ appearing to local Indians, although in reality the Spanish probably chose a dark wood for the statue hoping that a dark-skinned Christ would help their campaign to convert the Indians. Actually, Esquipulas had been the site of religious ceremonies before the Spanish arrived and the Maya had more than one black deity.

Villages throughout Guatemala choose at least one person from their community to represent them at the festival. On January 15, people wait in enormous lines outside the church for their chance to light a devotional candle at the statue, which is believed to possess miraculous powers. This legend gained popularity after the bishop of Guatemala claimed to have been cured of an illness in 1737.

Lighting candles is the culmination of the pilgrimage undertaken by many Guatemalans each year. The Esquipulas Pilgrimage is a solemn occasion, given over to prayer and religious devotion.

CORN FESTIVALS

In a land where successful corn planting and harvesting is crucial to the livelihoods of the people, it is not surprising that many ceremonies and festivals are associated with corn. Before planting takes place, special masses are said in the local church. On the night before the first seeds are planted, incense is often burned in the fields and candles are lit in homes. The following morning the candles are placed in the fields, and after sowing, celebratory meals are enjoyed. The first seeds are traditionally sown by the oldest member of the family.

The planting season is during March and April. The months from October to December are devoted to corn harvesting and more celebrations usually take place in this period. During harvesting great attention is given to the selection of seeds for the next planting cycle.

In some villages, particularly large ears of corn are tied to the side of a fireworks rocket and launched into the sky. If all goes well and the rocket soars to a great height, that is taken as a good sign that the year will yield a bountiful corn harvest. Fireworks are lit again when processions carry the harvested corn back to the village, and the happy occasion is marked by yet another feast.

CEREMONY OF THE EIGHT MONKEYS

One of the Mayan calendars is based on a cycle of 260 days, composed of 13 smaller cycles of 20 days each. The 261st day is the Mayan New Year.

Corn plays an important role in the life and legends of Guatemalan people. More than just a staple food, it is considered in Indian mythology to be the source of human life.

The New Year is celebrated in a festival known as the Ceremony of the Eight Monkeys. The village of Momostenango in the western highlands is famous for observing this ancient ceremony. Originally a pagan festival, it has now merged with Roman Catholicism, and celebrations begin with a church service on the eve of the New Year.

At dawn the next day, villagers make their way to a nearby hill where altar mounds are located. These mounds, measuring between 3 and 10 feet (1 and 3 m) high, are topped with offerings of broken pottery. A shaman stands behind each altar and receives the offerings on behalf of the gods. Each Indian giving an offering utters a request to the gods, and the shaman burns wafers of sacred incense to accompany the request. This ceremony continues until dusk and then moves to another holy site in the vicinity, where the shamans pray and burn incense throughout the night.

Momostenango means "the place of the altars." The town had its name long before the Spanish arrived, illustrating just how ancient the ceremony really is.

Originally a Mayan ceremony, the pagan Ceremony of the Eight Monkeys has now been merged with the largely Roman Catholic community and carried out at graves such as these.

FOOD

FOR CENTURIES, CORN has been an essential part of life in Guatemala. Beans and squash are also important. Most Guatemalans would not survive without these three crops. For many Indians, beans provide a good source of protein and are eaten with corn tortillas (tor-TEE-yahs) almost every day. Meat is too expensive for many people and is often consumed only on special occasions. In rural areas, people produce most of what they eat. Food that does need to be purchased is often paid for by using the proceeds from secondary crops such as other vegetables, which are grown primarily for their cash value.

The type of cuisine that is available in urban areas is more varied. Guacamole, made from mashed avocados and onions is popular, as are rolls made from steamed corn dough and filled with beans or a small amount of meat. Other foods such as pork chops, grilled chicken, and hamburgers are also available to those who can afford them. The most popular and affordable dish is beans served with rice. It usually is served as a standard item in *comedors*. A *comedor* (com-e-DOR) is a cafélike eating establishment that serves inexpensive ordinary food. There is usually no menu because local people simply know or ask for what is available. Restaurants as well as *comedors* are easily accessible in larger towns and cities, but in the villages, most people prefer to eat at *comedors* located close to the main market.

A typically large home-style breakfast consists of eggs, beans, and tortillas, sometimes accompanied by a sour cream sauce. Breakfast in the highlands may also include a bowl of *mosh* (MOSH), a mixture of oats and milk. For most families, the main meal of the day is lunch, and though beans may be included, the tortilla forms the basis of the meal. Bananas also are often consumed, always available.

Above: **People enjoy dining in colorful restaurants in Antigua.**

Opposite: **A bustling Guatamalan market day. Rows of fresh local fruits and vegetables make the place a truly gastronomical wonderland to shop in.**

125

FAST FOOD, GUATEMALAN STYLE

The fast food establishments found in so many parts of the world are a familiar sight in Guatemalan cities. If they are not as common as in North American cities, it is mainly because most people cannot afford to eat in such establishments.

Cheap fast food takes a different form in Guatemala and is ideal for the kind of people who are constantly on the move. Large numbers of migrant workers, combined with the prohibitive cost of private transportation, means that regional buses are usually packed. When these buses make a stop, especially in the busier transportation hubs, street vendors appear out of nowhere with a range of fast food items and drinks. They crowd around the open windows of the buses, offering quick snacks as well as complete meals at nearby tables.

The most common fast food snack is the *tamal* (TAM-al), or tamale, made from cooked cornmeal and perhaps stuffed with tomatoes, meat, and seasonings, then wrapped in a banana leaf. Stuffed peppers are another favorite snack item.

TORTILLAS AND BEANS

For the average Guatemalan, tortillas and beans are traditional food staples. Tortillas are thin circular pancakes made from corn and are usually topped with beans and other vegetables, or wrapped to form a type of sandwich encasing a juicy filling of beans. They may be seasoned with chili salsa or plain salt. In rural areas, tortillas are traditionally freshly made early each morning, but machine-made versions are becoming more common, especially in towns. Tortillas need to retain their moisture in order to taste good, so they are kept wrapped in a slightly wet cloth. Sometimes tortillas are dried out instead. Toasting these pancakes when they are still fresh helps to retain a crisp tastiness.

Beans cooked in different ways—fried or boiled—are often eaten with tortillas, but they also make a delicious meal on their own when cooked with chilies. When eaten with tortillas, they are boiled until soft and mashed into a paste, which is then refried. The other method of preparing beans is to boil them and dish them up hot in their own juice.

SOME GUATEMALAN SPECIALITIES

caldo	meat-based broth
ceviche	raw fish salad marinated and "cooked" in lime juice
chile relleno	stuffed pepper
chuchito	stuffed corn dumpling
enchilada	a flat, crisp tortilla piled with salad or meat
mosh	porridge of oats and milk
pan de coco	coconut bread
pepian	stew of chicken, peppers, potatoes, and pumpkin seeds
quesadilla	toasted or fried tortilla, with cheese
taco	rolled and stuffed tortilla
tamale	stuffed, seasoned cornmeal dough, boiled or steamed
tapado	fish stew with plantain and vegetables

CHILIES

In the ancient book *Popol Vuh*, chilies are named as a food made by the gods and enjoyed by the first people. No wonder their popularity is unsurpassed! A bowl of chilies, raw or pickled, is a must on a restaurant table.

Chilis add a splash of color and a dash of spice into most Guatemalan dishes.

Ancient Mayan rulers enjoyed meals topped with chocolate sauce made from cocoa beans. The careless extravagance of that practice is best appreciated when one realizes that the common people of that time used cocoa beans as a form of currency.

A wide variety is available, and colorful mounds of red and green chili peppers brighten many Guatemalan markets. They are used to make various sauces that flavor meals, and their versatility has given them a special place in kitchens across Latin America.

Various flavors are possible, due to the peppers' different characteristics as well as their varied cooking methods. Generally, the longer the chilies are cooked, the more intense the taste. Many restaurants in Guatemala include a guide informing the diner how spicy each dish is according to the amount and type of chilies it contains. If a symbol of a man with fire exploding from his mouth and ears appears beside the name of a dish, be warned! The diner can be certain it will contain the hottest chilies that were at the cook's disposal.

DRINKS

The most popular nonalcoholic drinks are coffee and cocoa. Coffee is usually drunk with sugar and is surprisingly weak, considering the high quality of beans produced on the large Guatemalan plantations.

Tea is another well-liked beverage. It is usually taken without milk. A number of fresh fruit and vegetable juices are also widely available. Other drinks can be found only in certain areas. In the highlands, there is a warm and watery concoction made from corn or rice, flavored with sugar, honey, cardamom, or even powdered chili.

Beer was introduced by German immigrants, who came to the country to grow coffee in the late 19th century. The brew is a popular choice for many Guatemalans today. There are two main brands of lager whose names translate into "goat" and "rooster."

Aguardiente (ag-wahr-de-EN-tay)—a strong drink made from sugarcane—is also known as "white eye." Indians sometimes pour a small amount of it over the statue of the saint they are praying to. *Aguardiente* and *ron* (RON), or rum, are the most commonly found strong alcohol varieties in the country. There are many different qualities of rum available. The less expensive brands are sometimes mixed with soft drinks, partly to disguise the poor taste.

NON-INDIAN CUISINE

Ladino culture has influenced Guatemalan food, although that contribution is by no means only Spanish in character. The rich tastes of Mexican cuisine are also evident. Hamburgers and steak—favorite meals in the United States and Europe—are increasingly popular in the towns and cities. Indeed, a Ladino meal without meat is almost as uncommon as an Indian meal with meat.

A man holding up plates of fried chicken and french fries. Local fast food chains such as this provide tasty quick meals for those who can afford them.

One of the more famous Guatemalan regional dishes is chicken served in a spicy sauce made from pumpkins. In recent years, a dish called *chao mein* (CHOW MANE) has become popular with Ladinos. Although it consists of vegetables and rice, there is little resemblance to the Chinese-American dish called chow mein.

Mainly in the cities, especially Guatemala City, a diner might find a variety of food styles other than traditional Indian dishes. In rural areas and smaller towns, the ever-present corn- and vegetable-based diet of the Indian population dominates, though some interesting regional variations are found.

CHICKEN WITH PINEAPPLE (POLLO EN PIÑA)

Serves 6

3 lbs (1.5 kg) chicken, medium-sized pieces
2 tablespoons (30 ml) vegetable or olive oil
1 medium-sized onion, chopped
2 garlic cloves, minced
1 can (20 ounces/625 ml) of unsweetened pineapple chunks, drained
  (or 20 ounces fresh pineapple)
2 tablespoons (30 ml) of vinegar
½ cup (4 ounces/125 ml) of sherry
¼ teaspoon (1.25 ml) of ground cinnamon
¼ teaspoon (1.25 ml) of ground cloves
1 teaspoon (5 ml) of salt
Pinch of pepper
2 medium-sized tomatoes, chopped

Heat oil in a large skillet and cook chicken over medium-high heat for 15 minutes. It should be brown on all sides. Then remove the chicken, and sauté onion and garlic in the remaining oil until tender. Return the chicken to the skillet. In a small bowl, mix the pineapple chunks and all the remaining ingredients except the tomatoes and add to the chicken. Bring the mixture to a boil, then reduce heat, cover, and simmer for 20 minutes. Add tomatoes and simmer mixture uncovered for another 15–20 minutes. Serve hot with rice.

GUATEMALAN CORN CAKE

16 servings

1 package cake mix
1 package vanilla instant pudding mix
½ cup (4 ounces, 125 ml) vegetable oil
1 can (8.5 ounces, 265 g) creamed corn, mashed and strained before adding milk, if
  necessary, to the corn to make a full cup (8 ounces, 250 ml)
4 large eggs
1 teaspoon (5 ml) pure vanilla extract
Confectioners' sugar

Add all the ingredients to a mixer bowl and blend well at medium speed for 2 minutes. Pour the mixture into a greased tube pan. Place in an oven preheated to 350°F (180°C). Let it bake for 55 minutes. Insert a toothpick into the cake. The cake is done when the toothpick comes out clean without any batter sticking to it. Let the cake cool for 15 minutes and then turn the pan upside down onto a cooling rack to remove the cake. Let it rest there for another 15 minutes. Dust with confectioners' sugar for decoration.

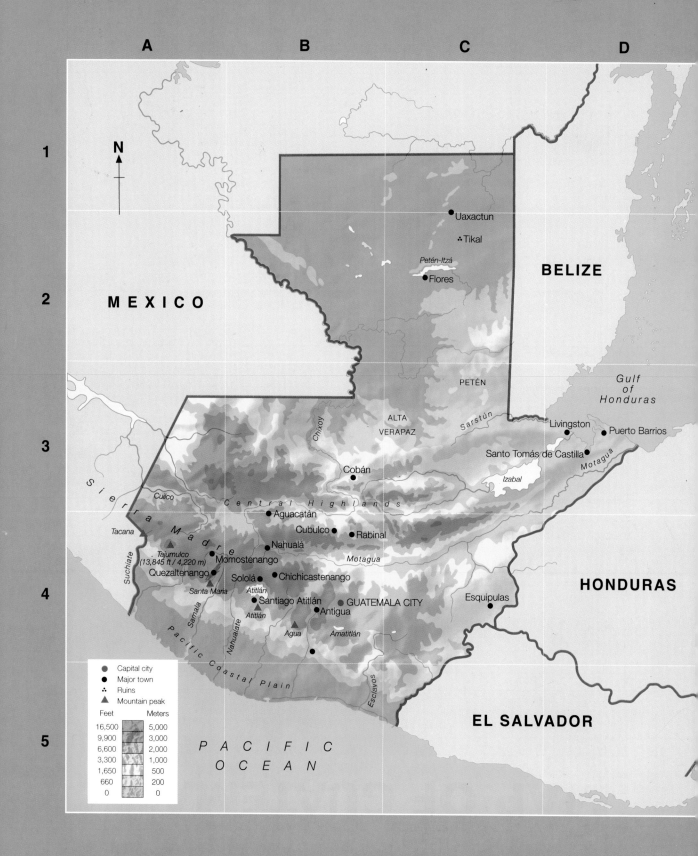

MAP OF GUATEMALA

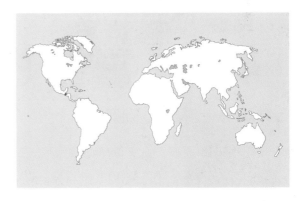

ECONOMIC GUATEMALA

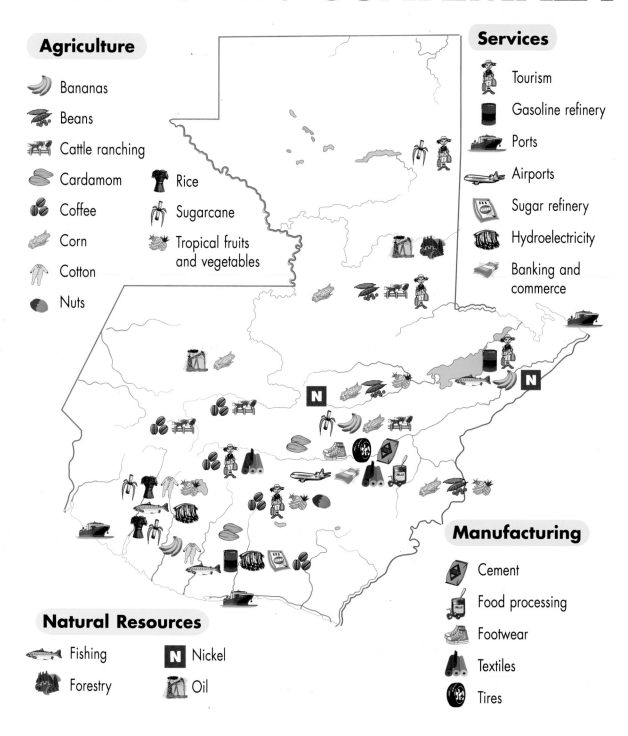

Agriculture

- 🍌 Bananas
- Beans
- Cattle ranching
- Cardamom
- Coffee
- Corn
- Cotton
- Nuts
- Rice
- Sugarcane
- Tropical fruits and vegetables

Services

- Tourism
- Gasoline refinery
- Ports
- Airports
- Sugar refinery
- Hydroelectricity
- Banking and commerce

Manufacturing

- Cement
- Food processing
- Footwear
- Textiles
- Tires

Natural Resources

- Fishing
- Forestry
- N Nickel
- Oil

ABOUT
THE ECONOMY

OVERVIEW
Since the civil war ended in 1996, Guatemala has enjoyed a steady influx of foreign investments. In 2006 the Central American Free Trade Agreement (CAFTA) between the United States and Guatemala and other countries came into effect. The agricultural sector employs half of Guatemala's labor force and generates almost a quarter of national revenues. To reduce customary reliance on plantation crops such as coffee and bananas, Guatemala is diversifying into agricultural products such as other fruits and vegetables. Tourism and remittances from overseas workers provide much-needed foreign income. Nevertheless, unequal wealth distribution and the rural-urban divide continue to threaten social cohesion. Over half of Guatemalans live in poverty.

GROSS DOMESTIC PRODUCT (GDP)
$62.53 billion (2007 estimate)

GDP GROWTH
5.6 percent (2007 estimate)

INFLATION RATE
6.8 percent (2007 estimate)

LAND USE
Arable land 13.2 percent, permanent crops 5.6 percent, other 81.18 percent

CURRENCY
Guatemalan quetzal (GTQ), circulated in values of 100, 50, 20, 10, 5 and 1.
100 centavos = GTQ 1
7.6 GTQ = US$1

NATURAL RESOURCES
Petroleum, nickel, rare woods, fish, hydropower

AGRICULTURAL PRODUCTS
Bananas, beans, cardamom, coffee, corn, sugarcane, fruits, vegetables, chickens, livestock (cattle, pigs, sheep)

INDUSTRY
Sugar, chemicals, metals, petroleum, rubber, furniture, textiles and clothing, tourism

MAJOR EXPORTS
Coffee, sugar, bananas, cardamom, fruits, vegetables, clothing, petroleum

MAJOR IMPORTS
Fuel, machinery, construction materials, electricity, grains, fertilizers

MAIN EXPORT PARTNERS
United States 44.6 percent, El Salvador 11.9 percent, Honduras 7.2 percent, Mexico 5.2 percent (2006 estimates)

MAIN IMPORT PARTNERS
United States 33.3 percent, Mexico 8.8 percent, China 6.5 percent, El Salvador 5.3 percent, South Korea 4.9 percent (2006 estimates)

WORKFORCE
3.9 million (2007 estimates)
Agriculture 50 percent, industry 15 percent, services 35 percent

UNEMPLOYMENT RATE
3.2 percent (2005 estimate)

POPULATION BELOW POVERTY LINE
56.2 percent (2004 estimate)

FOREIGN RESERVES
$4.1 million (2007 estimate)

CULTURAL GUATEMALA

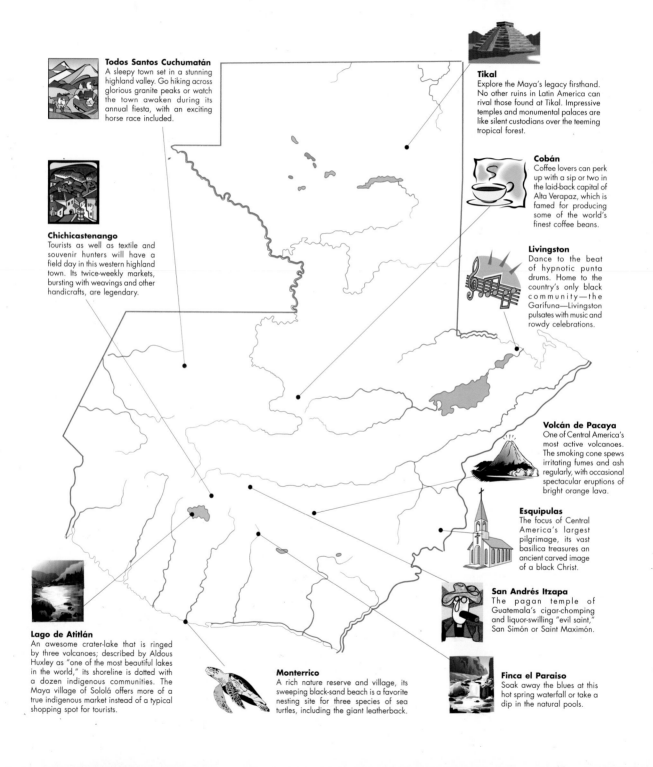

Todos Santos Cuchumatán
A sleepy town set in a stunning highland valley. Go hiking across glorious granite peaks or watch the town awaken during its annual fiesta, with an exciting horse race included.

Chichicastenango
Tourists as well as textile and souvenir hunters will have a field day in this western highland town. Its twice-weekly markets, bursting with weavings and other handicrafts, are legendary.

Tikal
Explore the Maya's legacy firsthand. No other ruins in Latin America can rival those found at Tikal. Impressive temples and monumental palaces are like silent custodians over the teeming tropical forest.

Cobán
Coffee lovers can perk up with a sip or two in the laid-back capital of Alta Verapaz, which is famed for producing some of the world's finest coffee beans.

Livingston
Dance to the beat of hypnotic punta drums. Home to the country's only black community—the Garífuna—Livingston pulsates with music and rowdy celebrations.

Volcán de Pacaya
One of Central America's most active volcanoes. The smoking cone spews irritating fumes and ash regularly, with occasional spectacular eruptions of bright orange lava.

Esquipulas
The focus of Central America's largest pilgrimage, its vast basilica treasures an ancient carved image of a black Christ.

San Andrés Itzapa
The pagan temple of Guatemala's cigar-chomping and liquor-swilling "evil saint," San Simón or Saint Maximón.

Lago de Atitlán
An awesome crater-lake that is ringed by three volcanoes; described by Aldous Huxley as "one of the most beautiful lakes in the world," its shoreline is dotted with a dozen indigenous communities. The Maya village of Sololá offers more of a true indigenous market instead of a typical shopping spot for tourists.

Monterrico
A rich nature reserve and village, its sweeping black-sand beach is a favorite nesting site for three species of sea turtles, including the giant leatherback.

Finca el Paraiso
Soak away the blues at this hot spring waterfall or take a dip in the natural pools.

ABOUT
THE CULTURE

OFFICIAL NAME
Republic of Guatemala

FLAG DESCRIPTION
Two equal bands of light blue flank a white band containing a coat of arms in the center. Framed by a wreath, the coat of arms includes a green and red quetzal—the national bird—together with a scroll that bears Guatemala's independence date atop a pair of crossed rifles and swords.

INDEPENDENCE
September 15, 1821

CAPITAL
Guatemala City

MAJOR CITIES
Quezaltenango, Antigua, Chichicastenango, Escuintla, Flores, Puerto Barrios

POPULATION
13 million (2008 estimate)

BIRTHRATE
28.6 births per 1,000 Guatemalans (2008 estimate)

DEATH RATE
5.2 deaths per 1,000 Guatemalans (2008 estimate)

POPULATION GROWTH RATE
2.1 percent (2008 estimate)

LIFE EXPECTANCY
69.9 years (2008 estimate)

ETHNIC GROUPS
Ladino (mestizo—mixed American Indian and Spanish or European) 59.4 percent, K'iche 9.1 percent, Kaqchikel 8.4 percent, Mam 7.9 percent, Q'eqchi 6.3 percent, Mayan 8.6 percent, indigenous non-Mayan 0.2 percent. Others 0.1 percent (2001 estimate)

RELIGION
Roman Catholicism 59.3 percent, Protestantism 40 percent, others 0.7 percent

MAIN LANUAGES
Spanish (official language) 60 percent, 23 officially recognized indigenous languages 40 percent

LITERACY
69.1 percent: male 75.4 percent, female 63.3 percent (2002 census)

MAJOR FESTIVALS AND HOLIDAYS
New Year (January 1), Semana Santa (seven days of Holy Week leading to Easter), Labor Day (May 1), Army Day (June 30), Independence Day (September 15), Columbus Day (October 12), Revolution Day (October 20), All Saints' Day (November 1), All Souls' Day (November 2), Immaculate Conception (December 8), Christmas (December 25)

TIME LINE

IN GUATEMALA	IN THE WORLD
2600 B.C. Start of Maya culture in Central America.	
A.D. 600 Construction of Tikal begins.	**A.D. 600** Height of the Mayan civilization
900 Maya mysteriously abandon Tikal and major cities.	**1000** The Chinese perfect gunpowder and begin to use it in warfare
1523 Spanish explorer Pedro de Alvarado invades Guatemala.	
1524 Alvarado establishes capital at Tecpán, Iximché.	
1527–40 Spanish conquest of Guatemala proceeds. Roman Catholic Church is established.	**1530** Beginning of transatlantic slave trade organized by the Portuguese in Africa
1541 Alvarado dies. A new capital is founded at Antigua.	**1558–1603** Reign of Elizabeth I of England
1600s Spanish colonial rule is entrenched throughout Guatemala as the power of the church grows.	**1620** Pilgrims sail the *Mayflower* to America
1697 The last of the independent Mayas fall to the Spanish colonizers.	
1750s Coffee culture is introduced to Guatemala.	
1773 A massive earthquake destroys the capital at Antigua.	
1776 Guatemala City becomes the country's capital.	**1776** U.S. Declaration of Independence
1821 Guatemala declares independence from Spain and joins the United Provinces of Central America federation.	
1847 Guatemala becomes an independent republic.	
1870s First liberal revolution results in Rufino Barrios becoming president. Start of the coffee boom.	**1869** The Suez Canal is opened.
1906 Railway construction to the Pacific coast is completed.	**1914** World War I begins.

IN GUATEMALA	IN THE WORLD
1930 Height of the banana boom cements United Fruit Company's immense power in Guatemala.	
	1939 World War II begins.
1944 President Jorge Ubico is deposed in the October Revolution.	**1945** The United States drops atomic bombs on Hiroshima and Nagasaki.
1954 CIA-backed military coup ends Jacobo Arbenz Guzmán's presidency and launches a series of military dictatorships.	**1957** The Russians launch Sputnik
1960s Start of Guatemala's civil war.	**1966–69** The Chinese Cultural Revolution
1967 Guatemalan writer Miguel Ángel Asturias wins the Nobel Prize in Literature.	
1976 Massive earthquake kills 23,000 Guatemalans and leaves a million homeless.	
1986 Return to civilian rule under elected President Vinicio Cerezo.	**1986** Nuclear power disaster at Chernobyl in Ukraine
1991 Guatemala recognizes the independence of Belize. Peace talks between the government and guerrillas take place.	**1991** Breakup of the Soviet Union
1992 Rigoberta Menchú wins Nobel Peace Prize for advancing indigenous rights.	
1996 Signing of Peace Accords ends Guatemala's 36-year civil war.	**1997** Hong Kong is returned to China.
1998 Hurricane Mitch rips through Central America, killing hundreds of Guatemalans and destroying banana crops.	**2001** Terrorists crash planes in New York, Washington, D.C., and Pennsylvania. **2003** War in Iraq begins.
2004 Óscar Berger becomes president and slashes the number of armed forces. Portillo flees to Mexico.	
2006 The CAFTA (Central America Free Trade Agreement) treaty with the United States becomes effective.	
2008 Álvaro Colom Cabelleros takes office as Guatemala's president.	

GLOSSARY

aguardiente (ag-wahr-de-EN-tay)
A strong alcoholic drink made from sugarcane.

alfombras (al-FOM-bras)
Spanish for carpet, used to describe the patterned street "carpet" that is made from sawdust and flower petals during Holy Week processions.

bajos (BAA-hos)
Small depressions in the land that collect moisture.

cofradías (coh-frah-DEE-ass)
Religious brotherhoods composed of lay members.

comedor (com-e-DOR)
An eating establishment similar to a café that serves inexpensive home-style food.

fiesta
A party, festival.

glyph
A sculptured symbol or character, the literary tool of the ancient Maya.

huipil (WEE-pil)
Overblouse or tunic, worn tucked into a skirt.

Ladino
People of mixed Spanish-Indian ancestry; mestizo.

ladinization
Term describing the growing influence of Ladino (Western) lifestyle on Indian culture.

laterization
Process in which bare soil is exposed to intense heat and rain, eventually hardening into bricklike substances.

milpa (MIL-pa)
An Indian farmer's plot of land, used mainly for the growing of corn.

mosh (MOSH)
Porridgelike mixture of oats and milk that is eaten for breakfast in the highlands.

Popol Vuh (poh-POL VOO)
An ancient Mayan text written by Indians that has survived in the form of a Spanish translation.

Semana Santa
Holy Week, the most important seven days for religious festivals in Guatemala, leading to Easter.

shamans
Holy people, or priests, considered capable of reaching and interceding with supernatural powers.

stela
Archaeological term referring to an upright pillar, usually inscribed for commemorative purposes.

tamal (tam-AL)
A popular snack made from cornmeal and boiled after being wrapped in a banana leaf.

Tikal
One of the largest Mayan cities and ceremonial centers, located in the Petén rain forest.

tortillas
Thin circular corn flat bread, the primary staple in the diet of Guatemalan Indians.

traje (TRAH-hay)
Traditional dress.

FURTHER INFORMATION

BOOKS

Asturias, Miguel Ángel. *Men of Maize: The Modernist Epic of the Guatemalan Indians*. Pittsburgh, PA: The University of Pittsburgh Press (Pittsburgh Editions of Latin American Literature), 1995.

Hecht, Ann. *Textiles from Guatemala*. London: The British Museum Press, 2001.

Janson, Thor. *Maya Nature: An Introduction to the Ecosystems, Plants and Animals of the Mayan World*. Champaign, IL: Vista Publications, 2001.

Martin, S. and N. Grube. *Chronicle of the Maya Kings and Queens*. New York: Thames and Hudson, 2007.

Menchú, Rigoberta. *I, Rigoberta Menchú—An Indian Woman in Guatemala*. New York and London: Verso, 1984.

Pendergrast, Mark. *Uncommon Grounds: The History of Coffee and How It Transformed Our World*. New York: Basic, 2000.

Wilkinson, Daniel. *Silence on the Mountains: Stories of Terror, Betrayal and Forgetting in Guatemala*. New York: Houghton Mifflin, 2002.

WEB SITES

Amnesty International: Human Rights Social Issues. (Select Guatemala.) www.amnesty.org

Country Overview. CIA World Factbook. https://www.cia.gov/library/publications/the-world-factbook/geos/gt.html

Earthquakes: Case Studies. http://library.thinkquest.org/C003603/english/earthquakes/casestudies.shtml

Guatemala. Economic and Environmental Issues. http://encarta.msn.com/encyclopedia_761556126/Guatemala.html

Guatemalan Lakes. Environment. www.enjoyguatemala.com/lakes.htm

Guatemalan National Symbols. www.stanford.edu/group/arts/guatemala/discovery/geography/symbols.htm

Nature Conservancy in Guatemala. www.nature.org/wherewework/centralamerica/guatemala/work/art21570.html

Parks Watch. www.parkswatch.org

Petén Region and Maya Biosphere Reserve. www.nmnh.si.edu/botany/projects/cpd/ma/ma13.htm

Recipe Zaar. Guatemalan Chicken with Pineapple. Recipes. www.recipezaar.com/78150

Recipe Zaar. Guatemalan Corn Cake. www.recipezaar.com/26052

USAID: Guatemala—Environment Summary. www.usaid.gov/locations/latin_america_caribbean/environment/country/guatemala.html

World Bank, The. World Development Indicators 2007. www.worldbank.org/data/wdi2001/pdfs/tab3_6.pdf

World Heritage Centre: Tikal National Park. http://whc.unesco.org/en/list/64

MUSIC

Guatemalan musical style, from the ancient Maya to present times. *Music of Guatemala*. Historia General de Guatemala

National Anthem of Guatemala. www.stanford.edu/group/arts/guatemala/discovery/geography/symbols.htm#National_Anthem

BIBLIOGRAPHY

O'Kane, Trish. *In Focus—Guatemala: A Guide to the People, Politics and Culture.* Northampton, MA: Interlink, 2003.

Pan American Health Organization. *Health in the Americas: 1998 Edition, Volume II, Guatemala.* Washington, DC: PAHO, 1999.

Stewart, Ian. *The Rough Guide to Guatemala.* London, UK: Rough Guides, 2006.

Thames and Hudson. *Sacred Symbols: The Maya.* London, UK: Thames and Hudson, 1996.

World Bank, The. *Poverty in Guatemala.* Washington, DC: World Bank, 2004.

World Health Organization. *Global Water Supply and Sanitation Assessment 2000 Report: Latin America and the Caribbean.* Geneva, Switzerland: WHO, 2001.

PAPERS

Edwards, Melissa and Carlos Morales. "WWF-Central America Freshwater Program Case Study." Gland, Switzerland: World Wildlife Fund, 2004.

Obregón, Mireya. "A Step Forward but Still a Long Way to Go: Guatemala." Paris: EFA Global Monitoring Report, 2003.

INDEX